A Short History of Prince Edward Island

Dr. Ed Whitcomb

From Sea to Sea Enterprises

Ottawa

Library and Archives Canada Cataloguing in Publication

Whitcomb, Dr. Edward A.
A Short History of Prince Edward Island / Ed Whitcomb.

Includes bibliographical references and index.
ISBN 978-0-9865967-1-1

1. Prince Edward Island – History. I. Title.

FC2611.W45 2010   971.7   C2010-902379-X

© From Sea To Sea Enterprises, 2010
2130 Dutton Crescent, Ottawa,
Ontario, Canada, K1J 6K4

Printed in Canada by Dollco Printing, Ottawa

Table of Contents

This Book is Dedicated to the

People of

Prince Edward Island

Preface

This is the eighth in a series of history books on Canada's ten provinces. The idea for this series first arose in 1969 when I moved to Nova Scotia. Being new to the province and knowing very little about it, I went looking for a short history book which would provide an outline of the development of my newly-adopted home. There was no such book. In fact, there were hardly any short histories of any of Canada's provinces. In 1975, I decided to write the sort of book I had been looking for, and began with my native province of Manitoba. Over 8,000 copies of that *Short History of Manitoba* have been sold, which suggests that I was not alone in wanting good, short provincial histories.

The project to write histories of all the provinces was delayed by family and career, but the Centennials of Alberta and Saskatchewan put the series back on track, and the short histories of those provinces were published in 2005. It made sense to continue with western and then central Canada so *British Columbia* was published in 2006, *Ontario* in 2007, *Nova Scotia* in 2009, and *New Brunswick* and *PEI* this year. The series will be completed when *Newfoundland and Labrador*, *Quebec*, and *Northern Canada* are published in 2011-12.

This *Short History of Prince Edward Island* is designed to provide the average reader with a quick but accurate survey of the broad outline of the Island's development. The emphasis is on the political developments that shaped the province as it is today, subjects such as the Natives, immigration and settlement, economic activities such as farming and fishing, and the attainment of responsible government. It explains the serious shortcomings of the Confederation arrangements, developments before World War I, prohibition, and the Depression. World War II and the post-war developments complete the account.

Every historian has a point of view that determines which of the thousands of issues he or she will discuss, which of the millions of facts he or she will mention, and what things he or she will emphasize or ignore. This is essentially a political history, with some reference to economic, constitutional, and social developments. It is a stand-alone history of the province, not a history of Canada as it unfolded in that province or a history of the localities that made up the province. It seeks to explain the Island's side in disputes between the province and the federal government. It is not "popular history," and does not include pictures. While the achievements of Islanders are documented, some criticisms are made of the heroes, politicians, and groups who have shaped the province. In short, it is but one perspective on a very fascinating and complex society. My greatest hope is that this small book will encourage others to read more and to write more on the dozens of issues and perspectives necessary to obtain a full understanding of any society's development.

This account ends with the government of Alex Campbell. Some readers would have wanted it to cover more recent developments, but there is a point where history merges into political science or journalism. While we know the broad outline of recent events, we do not have access to Cabinet decisions, correspondence, or the memoirs of most participants, and the secondary literature is far from comprehensive. Many issues are still current, some still the subject of sharp debate, and many views on them are more subjective than objective. Much research has to be done and many books and articles written before the recent past falls into a proper historical perspective.

Many people helped with the preparation of this book. A number of professors, editors, analysts, and experts read part or most of the text, and made many valuable corrections and suggestions. They include Dr. R. Matthew Bray, Dr. Phil Buckner, Leonard Cusack, Dr. Gerald Friesen, Dr. Daniel Livermore, Dr. Edward MacDonald, Margaret Poetschke, and Robert Poetschke. The cover design and map were prepared by Linda Turenne using a Natural Resources Canada map and the colours of the official flag of Prince Edward Island. Clifford Ford did the formatting and page layouts. John Colyer of Dollco Printers helped with the technical details. Most helpful of all was my wife, Kai, whose support and patience makes these books possible. I alone am responsible for the weaknesses that remain in the book.

Ottawa, May 2010.

Chapter One

Uncertain Beginnings, to 1805

Prince Edward Island is the smallest of Canada's ten provinces, the last Maritime province to be settled by Europeans, the sixth British North American colony to join Confederation, the most densely populated province, and one of the least ethnically diverse. It is also unique in terms of its geography. It is part of the St. Lawrence Plain, ground out of red sandstone which gives the soil its warm colour. It is a land of gentle, rolling hills, the highest only 140 metres above sea level, with a few cliffs, sand dunes and salt water marshes. Crescent-shaped, it is only 220 kilometres long and from four to 50 kilometres wide, with no place more than 20 kilometres from the sea. It measures a total of 5,660 square kilometres, 2,000 square miles, or 1,400,000 acres. PEI, as it is commonly known, or just "the Island," is separated from New Brunswick and Nova Scotia by the Strait of Northumberland, some 15-50 kilometres wide. The north coast is characterized by bays and sandy beaches, the south coast by many inlets, some of which cut the province into segments. Almost the entire surface is agricultural land of average quality, not sufficiently fertile to grow wheat but excellent for potatoes. The fishery and forests are its other major natural resources.

Prince Edward Island was discovered, explored, and settled by peoples who came to North America from Asia over 10,000 years ago. They called it Abegweit. These Mi'kmaq belonged to the Algonkian language group which stretches from the Rocky Mountains to the Atlantic Ocean. They were a semi-nomadic people, hunting moose, caribou, beaver, ducks, and geese; fishing for salmon, cod, and seals; and gathering oysters and clams. Warfare does not seem to have been a major factor in their lives, and they welcomed and traded with European visitors. They were not numerous and had become a small minority by the early nineteenth century.

The Island may have been known to European fishermen in the 15th century, but the first recorded sighting was by Jacques Cartier on his famous 1534 voyage. The name Île St. Jean was used by Samuel de Champlain when he explored it in 1604, and appeared on maps in the 1630s. That name was used in its English translation, St. John's Island, until 1799. In the seventeenth century, France made a large land grant to a nobleman on condition that he bring out settlers. Few came, and the grant was revoked and re-issued several times. After France lost mainland Nova Scotia to England in 1713, it encouraged French-speaking Catholic Acadian settlers from the Bay of Fundy region to move to Île St. Jean where they could provide both food and militia to assist in the defence of Cape Breton.

Those efforts essentially failed. In the early eighteenth century, there were only a few houses in the village of Fort La Joie at the mouth of the Hillsborough River (present-day Charlottetown), and a few hundred French and Acadian settlers scattered about. Agricultural production was restricted by crop failures and plagues of mice, and the colony was a drain on French resources rather than a source of support. Nevertheless, continued efforts at settlement and a high birth rate led to a gradual increase in population to around 1,000 when England and France went to war again in 1744. Intense efforts by France doubled that population by 1752.

Île St. Jean played virtually no role in that war, though New Englanders raided the coast and destroyed some houses. England took control in 1745 but gave it back to France three years later. In the next phase of warfare which began in 1754, English strategy included weakening France's position by deporting the Acadians from the Bay of Fundy region. As this program unfolded, hundreds and then thousands fled to Île St. Jean so that it had a population of perhaps 5,000 by the mid-1750s, mainly starving refugees. After England conquered Île St. Jean in 1758, the name was changed to St. John's Island, and it was made part of Nova Scotia. Colonel Lord Rollo and 500 soldiers were sent to take possession. They destroyed some houses and barns, deported over 3,000 Acadians, and forced many more back across the Strait of Northumberland.

The wars with France almost bankrupted England, and it had to devise a plan to develop the new colonies at little government expense. In 1764, Samuel Holland was sent to survey the island with a view to settlement. He divided it into three counties, Kings, Queens, and Prince, of roughly 500,000 acres each. They were subdivided into 67 townships of approximately 20,000 acres each, with their agricultural potential graded in three levels. Land was allocated for three county capitals, Georgetown in Kings, Charlottetown in Queens, and Princetown on Malpeque Bay for Prince County. Within each township, land was set aside for schools and churches, and 500 feet of land was reserved along the entire coast for the fishery. Holland's survey lines actually run 15 degrees west of true north producing a slight distortion on today's maps.

To many prominent Englishmen the acquisition of PEI seemed like a golden opportunity to become wealthy, and politicians, generals, admirals, businessmen, and land speculators coveted the fertile lands. One was the Earl of Egmont, First Lord of the Admiralty, who modestly proposed that the entire island be given to him. Instead, it was decided to give the 67 townships to about

100 applicants by means of a lottery held on July 23, 1767. The new proprietors agreed to three main conditions: they would bring one settler per 200 acres within 10 years; those settlers would be Protestants from outside the British Isles; and they would pay a tax known as a quit rent of two, four or six shillings per 100 acres depending on the quality of the soil. If these conditions were not met, the land was to revert to the Crown which could then grant it to someone else. That policy was not inappropriate, but the way it was administered would retard the province's development and dominate politics for a century.

Within a decade, one quarter of the grants had been sold by the original proprietors, suggesting that the main motivation of many applicants was speculation. Some of the remaining proprietors asked the British Government to make St. John's Island a colony separate from Nova Scotia. Since there were no settlers, government, nor infrastructure, this request had little justification other than giving enormous political power to the proprietors. It was granted, however, on May 30, 1769, suggesting that the British Government cared little about the fate of the little island colony. But it did care about expenses, so provincial status was made conditional on the new administration being financed entirely from quit rents. It was also made clear that if that revenue was not adequate, salaries would have to be reduced until the budget was balanced. Those mistaken policies created a poisonous and virtually hopeless administrative, political, financial, legal, and social situation which was not fully resolved until after Confederation.

On July 14, 1769, one of the new proprietors, Walter Patterson, was appointed Governor. It was an unfortunate choice because he had neither the experience nor the temperament for the position. In addition, as a proprietor he had a vested interest in acquiring more land and in avoiding the payment of his own quit rents, but he also had an interest in collecting quit rents from others since that paid his salary. From the beginning he was a friend of some proprietors and an enemy of others, a partner to some of the officials and an opponent of others, an agent of the British government and an opponent of some of its policies. As the years passed, the effects of his character weaknesses and of these contradictions accumulated.

Upon arrival in 1770, Patterson appointed a few people to his administration and began the daunting task of attracting settlers and building a province. Until they could collect some quit rents, Patterson and his officials were virtually without income and had to draw down their savings to survive. The government had no money to spend, and a British grant for churches and government buildings was used to pay part of the officials' salaries. A few settlers arrived along with a couple of proprietors, but within a very short period it became clear that most proprietors were not going to fulfill their obligations. It also became clear that some of the obligations were impractical - there was no source of Protestant settlers from outside the British Isles, and many of the first settlers were in fact Highland Scottish Catholics. It also became clear that the British government had no intention of enforcing the conditions. This was the beginning of an unfortunate political legacy in which governments passed laws, rules, and regulations and then failed to enforce them, breeding habits of lawlessness and disrespect for authority.

Under these uncertain circumstances, Governor Patterson called for the election of the province's first Assembly. On July 4, 1773, the Island's male Protestant voters gathered in Charlottetown to elect 18 Members of the Legislative Assembly (MLAs) to the first Assembly. It promptly passed a number of minor laws plus a major one to enforce the collection of quit rents. London vetoed that bill, creating a situation in which the provincial government could neither collect the taxes necessary for its proper functioning nor force landowners to develop their vacant lands. This "land question" soon became the main issue in Island politics.

By 1775, the population had increased to only 1,200, so Patterson left for England to deal directly with the issue. He convinced Parliament that quit rents could not cover the expenses of the administration, and Parliament agreed to pay a large part of the cost. He also confirmed that proprietors were to bring out settlers and pay quit rents or forfeit their land grants. During the five years Patterson spent in England, the colony languished and the administration deteriorated due to the death of some officials and the capture of several others by New England privateers during the American War of Independence.

Upon returning in 1780, Patterson set out to implement the land grant policy. The need was great. Warfare had reduced immigration, and there were no settlers in most of the townships. Few proprietors had paid any quit rents. Patterson's interests as a proprietor now conflicted with his responsibilities as Governor, and his administration of the policy reflected the worst traits in his character. He used a legal expedient known as distraint to seize a number of estates which could then be sold. The decision as to which lots would be seized was somewhat arbitrary as some proprietors who had brought out settlers lost their land, and some who had not were spared. Valuable land was more likely to be seized than marginal land. The "auction" of that land in November, 1781, was rigged to favour Patterson and his supporters. They paid nothing for the land, claiming the value of the property as compensation for the salaries still owed to them.

Some members of Patterson's Executive objected to the procedure, especially Chief Justice Peter Stewart, whose relations with Patterson were not helped by the intimate relationship between Patterson and Stewart's wife. The absentee landlords in London appealed to the Colonial Office on the grounds that they had done all they could to fulfill the conditions. They were joined by some of the proprietors resident in PEI and by some members of the PEI government itself, people who perhaps had not shared in the spoils. In 1783, the Colonial Secretary, Lord North, ordered Patterson to stop any further proceedings and wait for instructions. Those instructions were to provide a means by which proprietors who had lost land in 1781 could buy it back. If they did, they would have, in effect, paid their arrears, and if they did not, the new owners would have clear titles.

That, however, was not what Patterson wanted since he had now accumulated nearly 200,000 acres of property, close to one sixth of the entire colony. He ignored Lord North's instruction to have the new policy approved by the Assembly. He also attracted around 500 Loyalist immigrants and settled many of them on disputed lands. They became his political allies. Problems with obtaining clear title to land discouraged further Loyalist settlement, and PEI gained little from the flood of Loyalists that enriched Nova Scotia and created New Brunswick. In the spring of 1784, Patterson tried to address the legal and political quagmire he had created. He was not sure of his support in the Assembly so he called for new elections. Unfortunately for him, his opponents led by Chief Justice Stewart's son won a majority of the seats. The Assembly debated the land issue for 19 days and adjourned. Patterson then dissolved it, but before leaving, the members posted a public denunciation of Patterson for illegally appropriating land and money for his personal use. Patterson then dismissed Chief Justice Stewart and his friends from the Executive and called for new elections which his supporters won. By that time, the Colonial Office knew that he had ignored Lord North's instructions to present the new policy to the Assembly, and demanded an explanation. His argument that the policy contained too many errors to be presented to the Assembly fell on deaf ears in London, and in May, 1785, he was ordered to present an amended version to the Assembly.

Once more Patterson delayed, and in March 1786, he had the Assembly approve a motion confirming the sales of 1781. In June he was ordered to appear in London to explain his conduct, and Colonel Edmund Fanning was ordered to proceed from Nova Scotia to Charlottetown to take over the government. Patterson ignored the order, stayed in Charlottetown, and refused to hand power to Fanning on the argument that Fanning could be lieutenant governor only in Patterson's absence. Over the winter of 1786-7, both the current and future lieutenant governors struggled to assert their authority over officials who were forced to take sides. Fanning dissolved the Assembly and Patterson prorogued it, leaving the MLAs unsure of their status. In April 1787, the Colonial Office put an end to the farce by dismissing Patterson.

Edmund Fanning had many of the qualifications to be a good governor. He had a law degree from Yale, extensive experience in administration, a distinguished record as a Loyalist officer, friends in high places, and experience as lieutenant governor of Nova Scotia. The problems he faced on arrival, however, were almost as daunting as those faced by Patterson in 1770. Some were new and more complicated, including the political situation. Patterson had effectively divided the Island's elite into two factions: his own supporters and those of Chief Justice Stewart and his family. Both factions had the same goals, namely, to accumulate as much land, business, and government offices as possible, and to use their influence to advance those goals ruthlessly and even illegally. While both claimed to be protecting Island interests against absentee landlords, the agents of the latter were in fact part of both factions.

Fanning needed the support of at least part of one of the factions, and he turned first to Walter Patterson's brother. When that failed, he turned to Patterson's enemy, former Chief Justice Peter Stewart, whom he reinstated to office. In addition, he looked to his fellow Loyalists and brought more from Nova Scotia, giving them positions in the over-staffed and under-funded administration. He also gained the support of many absentee landlords by becoming their property agent, a clear conflict of interest.

Shortly after taking over in 1787, Fanning called an election. When the Patterson faction emerged with a majority, Fanning used violence and irregularities as excuses to void the results and call another election. The result was the same so, apart from a few special sessions, Fanning ignored the Assembly for the next four years. An important development, though, was that the single island-wide constituency was replaced by the three counties which elected four Assemblymen each, plus the three towns which elected two each. By 1790, Fanning was well enough established to call an election which returned a majority amenable to his views. With that support he saw no reason to call another election for 12 years.

Fanning met mixed results as he pursued his diverse goals. One was simply survival, at which he was very successful, governing the colony from 1787 to 1805. Like Patterson he had a major conflict of interest in that he wanted to administer all the island's property and people, but he also wanted to be a grand proprietor. In the pursuit of these goals, he was more successful with the latter, especially in taking over the land that Patterson had acquired. There were now three main elements to the land question, and Fanning faced different challenges and degrees of success with each of them. On the quit rent issue, the

Assembly kept passing laws, resolutions, and appeals to London with almost no effect. Instead, in 1802, the British government forgave most of the quit rents owed and gave the proprietors more time to pay. The absence of that revenue continued to cripple the colonial government, leaving the province with poor roads, education, justice, and administration.

The second was the issue of escheating vacant land, that is, reclaiming it because of the proprietors' failure to fulfill the conditions of the grant. A detailed study in 1797 indicated that 23 townships totalling 458,000 acres had no settlers, a further 23 covering 423,000 acres contained only 36 families, and another six townships covering 120,000 acres had only 50 families. The remaining 26 townships boasted a population of 3,856, so the terms of those grants had been satisfactorily met. The Assembly pointed out that Nova Scotia and New Brunswick were prosperous because vacant land had been escheated, re-sold, and developed, and it demanded the same for PEI. The British Government ignored the Assembly's petition for five years and then rejected it. Over the next half century, London consistently rejected attempts to solve the land problem by escheat, a policy that may have reflected concern with the situation in Ireland where the relations between landowners and tenants were far more complex and important. As old excuses for non-fulfilment of obligations became obsolete, new ones were invented and readily accepted by London. The provincial government succeeded, however, in seizing, and re-selling some land, and gradually some proprietors did foster immigration.

The third aspect of the land question was the relationship between tenants and landlords. Their interests were diametrically opposed, with the former wanting to avoid rent and buy land, and the latter wanting to keep their estates and maximize their revenue from rent. Some land was sold to tenants, and the proportion of farmers owning their own land increased steadily throughout the nineteenth century. Other tenants simply abandoned the land of the proprietors who had sponsored their immigration and squatted on vacant land. Most tenants stayed on the land they had been brought to and took advantage of the strong animosity against absentee landlords to demand that land be escheated and given or sold to them at low prices. On that issue the position of the proprietors was sound, and London supported them.

Chapter Two
Slow Development, 1805-1850

As the nineteenth century dawned, Prince Edward Island was a land of contrasts and contradictions. None of the elements of the land problem had been solved. Some of the proprietors had brought out large numbers of immigrants, and more had come without assistance. By 1805, the population had climbed to 7,000. There was still enough vacant land to keep the escheat issue alive for decades, but the proportion of cultivated land was increasing rapidly. The clearing of more and more forest created the primitive foundations of the lumber and shipbuilding industries, and customs revenue rose as imports steadily increased.

While most of the land was still owned by absentee landlords, more and more territory passed under the control of resident proprietors. Most settlers were tenant farmers subject to high rents and the threat of eviction. A few of them had acquired titles to land, more demanded titles, and their agitation against their landlords became a dominant theme of politics and economics.

The village of Charlottetown grew into a town and was linked to other villages by roads that were passable for most of the year. Across the island Highland and Lowland Scots probably made up a majority of the population. Englishmen, Irishmen, Acadians and a small number of Loyalists added to the ethnic mix. The Highlanders, Acadians and some of the Irish were Catholic. The Lowlanders were mostly Presbyterian, and the English and Loyalists were Anglican (Church of England), Methodist, or Baptist. The settlers continued with the back-breaking work of felling and removing trees, pulling up stumps, levelling and cultivating the soil, building houses and barns, and raising families. On the fringes a few Natives hunted and fished and looked for part-time work, their main challenge being simple survival. To avoid confusion with Saint John in New Brunswick and St. John's in Newfoundland, in 1799 the British Government changed the colony's name to Prince Edward Island in honour of Edward, fourth son of King George III and father of Queen Victoria.

Presiding over this confusion and adding considerably to it was the new Lieutenant Governor, Colonel Joseph Frederick Wallet DesBarres. At 83 years of age, he certainly had experience, including an unsuccessful stint as governor of the colony of Cape Breton. Upon his arrival, the Assembly asked him about the fate of the bills it had passed to deal with quit rents and escheat, bills which had not been approved by London. DesBarres had no knowledge of them, but soon sided with the proprietors on both issues. He informed London that in his view the original conditions were unrealistic, and it was not the fault of the proprietors that the island had not been settled. He also argued that if vacant land were escheated, tenants would buy it and move to it, thus vacating developed land which would then be subject to escheat. The Colonial Office required little convincing and vetoed both of the Assembly's bills.

The land issue dominated politics for most of DesBarres' term. It was complicated by competition for land and offices between two faction. One consisted of Fanning's supporters who occupied most of the offices when DesBarres arrived. A rival group known as the Loyal Electors was led by J.B. Palmer and consisted of Loyalists, non-proprietors, and political outsiders. DesBarres called an election in 1806 which maintained the Fanning faction in power but gave 5 of the 18 seats to the Loyal Electors. For years DesBarres tried to appoint officials and make decisions that would satisfy the absentee landlords, the local proprietors, and the various factions trying to manipulate the government for their own advancement. He failed, and was recalled in 1812.

His enemies and critics may not have rejoiced in the selection of the fourth Lieutenant Governor, Charles Douglass Smith, a man whose confidence, will-power, and arrogance were supported by neither experience nor political skills. Smith immediately clashed with the Assembly over his attempts to interfere with the militia. He ordered several soldiers to discipline their troops, but they refused to obey. His desire to dominate the militia seemed to be driven by paranoia, and he stationed most of the troops near his residence. Smith sided with the governing clique and condemned the Loyal Electors as Irish Catholics, Freemasons, and American republicans. He prorogued the new Assembly in 1813 and governed without it for four years. He gradually drove almost every group and faction into opposition, with the exception of the small Anglican minority which enjoyed a privileged position. Smith even managed to quarrel with their leaders.

In 1816, the Colonial Office looked once more at the question of quit rents. Proprietors were still not paying them, but land was being settled, and the population had risen to 15,000. The Colonial Office concluded once more that quit rents in arrears should be forgiven but that they should be collected from then on, subject to some new instructions. It was in Smith's interests to collect quit rents, and he arranged to do so in 1818, even though the new instructions had not yet arrived. Poor farmers paid up while rich proprietors ignored the threat. Smith then escheated several lots for non-fulfillment of terms, becoming the only Governor to use that power successfully. When the Colonial Office realized that Smith was actually collecting quit rents, it ordered him to stop, return the money collected, and not escheat any more property.

The Assembly was furious with Smith's actions, failures, and high-handed style. Those sentiments were documented in the traditional Address to the Lieutenant Governor. Smith refused to accept the Address, a refusal that was unprecedented and probably unconstitutional. He ordered the Assembly to adjourn itself or he would dissolve it, and his son, who shared his despotic tendencies and temper, smashed some windows in the Assembly's buildings. The Assembly imprisoned him, and Smith dissolved it thus freeing his son from imprisonment. When new elections produced an Assembly which was equally critical, Smith prorogued it for a further four years.

Smith again announced that quit rents had to be paid or property would be seized. Fearful of losing their land, many farmers sold cattle and personal possessions to make the payments. As usual, rich proprietors ignored the threat, and in January 1823, action was initiated against two of them. The situation rapidly deteriorated, and Smith asked the Governor of Nova Scotia to send troops. In March 1824, the Colonial Office ordered him to stop attempting to collect the quit rents and then recalled him.

Smith was replaced by Colonel John Ready, a man genuinely interested in developing the colony and in working with its politicians. He called elections which were won by the same clique that had given Smith so much trouble. The new Assembly attempted once more to solve the quit rent and revenue problems, but to no avail. By 1830, the population had reached 23,000, and the Assembly wanted to build a proper Legislative Building and other public works. Since sixty years of effort had produced little revenue from quit rents, it imposed a property tax of two shillings per 100 acres and asked the British Government to help abolish quit rents. London agreed to set aside quit rents for five years but not to abolish them. It would not, however, let the Assembly collect property taxes, so the financial problem remained unsolved.

A major step towards democracy was taken when Roman Catholics were given the vote in the British colonies, and five of them were elected in 1830. Almost 45% of the population was Catholic, and they accounted for a larger proportion of tenants who now had a stronger voice to support their grievances against the landlords. The main objection was simply the fact that they were working land that belonged to others. They did not want to pay rent, money that they could use to buy land. Proprietors gained enormously from the existing system and had little incentive to sell to those tenants who did manage to save some money. Tenants pressured the government to use the power of escheat to seize vacant lands, and the Assembly passed the necessary legislation in 1832. The new Lieutenant Governor, Aretas William Young, sent the Bill on to the Colonial Office which rejected it. The Assembly then passed a law imposing a property tax and the power to seize land if the taxes were not paid.

The proprietors correctly argued that this bill was simply another form of escheat, and the British authorities accordingly vetoed it. In 1834, Young died in office and was replaced by Sir John Harvey who was determined to solve the land problem. So was William Cooper, one of the leaders of a huge, radical movement that was determined to use the power of escheat to transfer land from proprietors to tenants. They now controlled the Assembly, and were prepared to force the issue. Harvey published the arguments Britain had provided him for rejecting the Assembly's escheat bills. That led to mass meetings bordering on rebellion. There were calls for the withholding of rents and for resistance to the proprietors. Petitions were signed saying that tenants were victims of fraud. Harvey labelled some of the resolutions treasonous. He asked the Assemblymen to repudiate the resolutions, and three MLAs who refused to do so were arrested by the other members.

Harvey then informed the Colonial Office that the rural resistance was over. He had introduced some positive reforms, and was promoted to the position of Lieutenant Governor of New Brunswick. Before he left, however, the Assembly was again demanding the escheat of vacant lands. Harvey's successor, Sir Charles Fitzroy, arrived to face a more determined Assembly which had passed a law taxing vacant land at twice the rate of developed land. It also provided figures showing that absentee landlords had paid less than 5% of the revenues collected in the previous 12 years. Fitzroy supported the Assembly's position as did Lord Durham who had been sent to the British North American colonies to examine the conditions that led to rebellion in Canada and discontent throughout the Maritimes.

In the 1838 election, Cooper and the Escheat Party won 18 of 24 seats and the new Assembly passed another bill calling for the confiscation of all vacant lands. The newly-created Legislative Council rejected it, and Fitzroy urged London to ignore further requests. The Colonial Secretary informed Fitzroy that London would not buy out the proprietors, and that it was unfair to enforce the original conditions. That rejection effectively destroyed the Escheat Party because it was now absolutely clear that bills and appeals to London would not succeed. That was confirmed when a party sympathetic to the proprietors won the 1842 election and gained control of the Assembly, the Executive Council and the Legislative Council. The next Lieutenant Governor, Sir Henry Huntley, disliked the colonial oligarchy and engaged in a number of petty squabbles with all three branches of government. When the 1846 election brought a chastened and more moderate group of Reformers back to power under George Coles, Huntley began to cooperate with them against the elite.

The land question then became entangled in the colonial movement towards Responsible Government. In the early nineteenth century, both the assemblies and the lieutenant governors wielded some power in the colonies. The assemblies controlled part of government revenue, which gave them some independence and influence over the lieutenant governor and his executive. The lieutenant governors had control over part of government revenue, and represented the British government which had sovereignty over the colonies. Within limits, lieutenant governors could accept or reject advice from elected Assemblymen, and could recommend that London not approve colonial legislation or actions. Responsible Government meant that on local issues, the power exercised by the lieutenant governors would be transferred to the colonial government or executive. Lieutenant governors would no longer appoint the executive, which would instead be based on the support of a majority of Assemblymen and be "responsible" to the Assembly. The pressure to achieve Responsible Government in the colonies came mainly from Canada and Nova Scotia, and PEI was swept up in the current by its geographical proximity.

There was little public pressure for Responsible Government, though some supporters of escheat probably thought it would strengthen their position. For the same reason some members of the elite were strongly opposed. Some MLAs were concerned that Responsible Government would strengthen the power of the leader of the dominant faction over the MLAs in that faction. Responsible Government also meant that the Executive would have to be replaced every time elections produced a new majority in the Assembly, which could lead to instability and problems with salaries and pensions.

By 1848, England decided to grant responsible government to Nova Scotia, New Brunswick, and Canada, but did not think PEI was ready. The new Lieutenant Governor, Sir Donald Campbell, fully agreed, arguing that the uneducated tenants would use such power to raise the escheat issue again and attack private property. He attempted to avoid implementing the reforms by calling an election in 1850, but the election was won by Coles' faction which was now known as the Liberals. Campbell offered the Liberals three of the nine seats in the Executive. Cole refused and the Assembly supported his position by a decisive 17 to 3 count. Campbell opposed Responsible Government until his death, but the next Lieutenant Governor, Sir Alexander Bannerman, was instructed to implement it. He did, and in April 1851, Coles formed the first government that was drawn from the elected Assembly.

Chapter Three

The Golden Age and the Rejection of Confederation, 1850-1864

At mid-century, Prince Edward Island was a vastly different colony from what it had been in 1800. The population had increased from 7,000 in 1805 to 47,000 in 1841, and would number 80,000 by 1861. Immigrants poured into the Island decade after decade, gradually settling most of the potential farmland. Catholic Highlanders and Presbyterian Lowland Scots constituted 45% of the population. Increasingly the waves of immigrants were poor Irish Catholics plus a sprinkling of Anglican and Presbyterian Irish. The Irish constituted 25% of the population, and the Island was over 70% Celtic. Englishmen constituted 20%, divided into Methodists, Anglicans and Baptists. Acadians did not prosper, but their numbers increased rapidly while the First Nations struggled to survive. Overall 55% of the population was Protestant and 45% Catholic. Gaelic was the Island's second language, French a distant third.

Socially, the Island reflected an interesting mix of classes. At the apex stood a few great proprietors in England, though their influence was diminishing. Local proprietors wielded great power over their tenants, and they held most of the positions in government and business. Over the decades these local families had become inter-related and mutually-supporting in their quest to maintain and expand their power and wealth. Prominent local merchants included the owners of businesses such as shipbuilding, brewing, or lumbering, while the petite bourgeoisie was involved in all the aspects of a bustling economy - law, medicine, teaching, preaching, exporting and importing, banking, construction, transportation, merchandising, and the manufacture of furniture, carriages, harness, leather goods, and textiles.

The largest concentration of population was in Charlottetown, which became a city in 1855 although its population was still only a few thousand. From there commerce spread out along red dirt roads to a dozen small towns such as Summerside, Georgetown, Tignish, St. Peters, Souris, and Montague. Most of these were ports with wharves, warehouses and a shipbuilding yard; a main street of stores, churches and a school; and a few huge houses for the local business elite plus perhaps a hundred small houses. The overwhelming majority of people were farmers, either freehold or tenant, with fishermen a distant second and workers a very small minority.

In 1850, Islanders were concerned with crops, prices, rents, land ownership, family, and religion. The implementation of Responsible Government kept the politicians busy, and people hoped that it would help resolve various problems such as the land question. Gradually, it became clear that, for government to work, most members of the Executive had to be Assemblymen. Others could, however, be drawn from the non-elected Legislative Council, which had been separated from the Executive in 1839. The size of the Executive created problems. It numbered twelve, but the Assembly contained only twenty-four MLAs, an inadequate pool from which to select the Executive. The solution to that problem was to expand the Assembly to thirty members and downsize the Executive to nine. Property qualifications for voting were reduced to the point that almost every adult male could vote.

Another problem was that a Legislative Council with a majority from one faction could block legislation coming from an Assembly dominated by another faction, as happened in 1854. That crisis was resolved when another election produced an Assembly of the same political persuasion as the Liberal Legislative Council. A subsequent crisis was resolved by the new government appointing additional Councillors until it had a majority there. The Conservatives began advocating the election of Councillors, a solution adopted in 1861, with voting limited to those who owned property worth more than £100. The lieutenant governors had considerable difficulty adjusting to the new system. Their power had been fading as that of the Assembly grew, but they continued to involve themselves in issues later regarded as local, particularly the calling of elections and the debates over Confederation.

At first political parties were too weak to properly support a system in which government relied on the continuous support of a majority in the Assembly. Religious issues cut across party lines and helped create shifting coalitions based on both parties. MLAs wanted to continue acting as individuals rather than as disciplined members of coherent parties. In general, however, the Conservatives tended to represent Protestants and landlords, while the Liberals were more representative of Catholics and tenants. By the 1880s, parties had become far more united and disciplined, partly because of their identification with their federal counterparts.

As the politicians struggled to make the political system work, they enjoyed one enormous advantage - the economy of PEI was booming. The Island's exports of potatoes, oats, cattle, fish, timber, and ships found ready markets in Britain, the other Atlantic colonies, the United States, and the West Indies. Shipbuilding became a major industry in numerous ports with almost 2,400 ships built between 1830 and 1864. Those ships were loaded with products, and both ship and cargo sold at the destination. The Island's products were so competitive that Britain's abandonment of tariff protection for colonial goods hardly affected the overall volume of exports, unlike other colonies that were more dependent on the British market. When Britain's North American colonies gained access to the American market with the Reciprocity Treaty of 1854, PEI's exports grew quickly, and the American Civil War created a huge demand for all of PEI's products.

These exports financed an import boom as new farms were carved out of the wilderness, old farms were bought up by tenants, towns grew quickly, infrastructure was built, small industries were established, and the overall population grew richer. Those imports produced a surge in customs revenue, and throughout the 1850's and 60s the provincial government had more than enough money to finance expenditure as well as reduce its debts. In 1855, the Bank of Prince Edward Island was founded to support all that economic activity. This was truly the Golden Age of PEI, and the fact that later generations of Islanders exaggerated the wonders of this period does not change that reality. After 1880, both the economic and the population growth rates declined, and outmigration replaced immigration as a major demographic factor. Islanders would become wealthier compared to their ancestors, but fall further and further behind the rest of North America.

Within this context Liberal Premier George Coles set out to address the colony's manifold problems. His first act was to strengthen the education system. All households in areas that had schools were to pay property taxes. A Board of Education took control of all schools that received government support. Each district built its own school, but the government paid teachers' salaries. School attendance doubled as over 150 schools were erected including a dozen for Acadians. Higher education was also advancing, with the Catholic institution at St. Andrew's College being replaced by St. Dunstan's College in 1857, and Central Academy becoming Prince of Wales College in 1860.

The schools were not without their problems, one of which concerned religion. There was broad agreement that passages from the Bible could be read at the beginning of the school day. Many Protestants wanted the teachers to "explain" those passages. Catholics objected because that meant that Catholic students would be exposed to Protestant religious teaching, and the proposal was discarded. In 1855, a new Normal School was opened, and the principal announced that there would be prayers and religious instruction. Catholics protested and the principal was forced to resign. Religious disputes toppled the Liberal government in 1858, and the question of religion in the schools remained a dominant political issue. The Conservatives in particular used religion to rally the Protestant majority against the perceived threat posed by the large Catholic minority.

The Liberal Government also launched another attack on the land issue. The Assembly passed a number of bills designed to use taxation to force proprietors to sell their vacant land. This had limited effect, but the Land Purchase Act of 1853 allowed the government to use its excess revenue to buy large estates. In this way the Worrell Estate of 81,000 acres was purchased and re-sold, as were the lands of Lord Selkirk's heirs. Between 1841 and 1861, the number of farmers owning their own land doubled, but over 60% of farmers were still tenants, and over half the island was still held by large proprietors. In 1860, the Conservative Government appointed a Commission representing the Assembly, the tenants and the proprietors. It recommended that the British Government guarantee a loan of £100,000 to buy out proprietors and that disputes over land go to arbitration. The proprietors objected to the recommendations and London ignored them.

While major problems remained to be addressed, PEI did not face the type of serious economic and political difficulties that would drive politicians in Britain's other North American colonies to seek some form of colonial union. In New Brunswick, Nova Scotia, and the Canadas exports never recovered from the loss of the British market, and in the Canadas, political deadlock was retarding economic progress. In the late 1850s, the movements for a union of the three Maritime provinces or for a greater union of all of Britain's North American colonies gained momentum. Neither was of much interest to Islanders. They valued their independence as a separate colony, had little contact with Canada, and were isolated from the mainland for five months of the year. Problems such as land ownership and religion were relatively more important to them. The British Government's failure to deal with the land issue had also made Islanders distrustful of distant governments.

In 1864, the Lieutenant Governor of New Brunswick proposed a conference of Maritime politicians to discuss a possible union. The need to reply triggered a discussion in the Assembly. Only one of twenty-four Assemblymen favoured the proposal, and other MLAs eloquently presented detailed arguments against both Maritime union and a larger federation. Most of PEI's trade was with Britain, the United States or overseas markets rather than with other British North American colonies. PEI would have a tiny representation and virtually no influence in any union. A Canadian federation would tax Islanders to build canals on the St. Lawrence-Great Lakes system and a railroad to the Pacific. While an Intercolonial railway was of considerable value to Nova Scotia and New Brunswick, it held little interest for Islanders. Other Maritime provinces would gain if the new central government took over their debts, but PEI had virtually no debt. Unlike the situation in other provinces, almost all of PEI's revenues came from tariffs which a central government would collect. In 1864, there was, in short, little reason for PEI to abandon its status as a separate colony.

The question, however, was whether to send a delegation to the proposed meeting, and that proposal was approved 18-9 in the Assembly. All the speakers in the Legislative Council opposed union but approved sending a delegation by a vote of 6-4. The debates in the two houses revealed such overwhelming opposition to union that the Lieutenant Governor's proposal was effectively killed. It was revived, however, when the Canadian Government asked if it could send observers to the proposed conference.

Nova Scotia Premier Charles Tupper then suggested that Charlottetown be the venue, and the date was set for September1, 1864. Arrangements proceeded for a conference, with Canadian delegates invited as observers. The Nova Scotia delegation was the first to arrive, but no one greeted them. Premier John Hamilton Gray greeted the Canadian delegates, but there was no accommodation for them because Charlottetown was hosting a big circus. Given PEI's strong opposition to Maritime Union, that idea was quickly dispensed with, and the Canadian delegation was invited to make the case for a larger union. John A. Macdonald and others wanted to create a unitary state, but that idea was completely unacceptable to PEI. The only realistic proposal left to discuss was that of a large, federal colony. Under that scheme, PEI would retain its independence as a province, its Assembly, and responsibilities for local issues, which were the ones of major interest to Islanders.

Island delegates expressed concern over the proposals for the transfer of responsibilities to the central government, the compensation the provinces would receive for the surrender of customs revenue, and the insignificant influence the Island would have in Ottawa. There was some discussion of the incentives that might attract Maritime colonies to join, including a possible loan of $800,000 so that PEI could buy out the remaining landlords. The delegates agreed on establishing a federation and on the general principles that would apply to that federation. They agreed to meet in Quebec City in October to work out the details. PEI decided to send a delegation, though there was little enthusiasm for the concept of Confederation.

At the Quebec Conference in October, all five delegations fought strenuously for the type of federation that met the needs of their respective colonies, and the PEI delegation distinguished itself advocating the interests of the Island. On the question of representation in the House of Commons, the principle of representation by population implied that PEI would elect five Members of Parliament (MPs), and that number of MPs would decline as a result of future settlement in western Canada. Some Islanders fought for strengthened representation in the Commons but lost. The Canadians proposed that the Senate should be based on equality between regions rather than equality between provinces or states as in the United States. It also proposed that Canada should be treated as two regions with twenty-four Senators each while the four Atlantic colonies should be treated as one with twenty-four Senators of which PEI would have four. The Maritime delegates accepted the concept of 24 Senators per region, but argued that the Maritimes was a distinct region and should have 24 while Newfoundland should have six. That was agreed, though Newfoundland soon opted out. The result was that 48 of the 72 Senators would come from central Canada which would then dominate the Senate as well as the Commons. The Canadian delegation proposed that Senators be appointed by the federal government, which meant they would not represent the regions. PEI delegates argued that they should be appointed by provincial governments and lost.

There was general agreement on the division of powers between federal and provincial governments. PEI argued that residual power over everything not specifically transferred to the new federal government should remain with the provinces, but lost that debate. Islanders argued that PEI should receive a greater compensation for the loss of customs revenue than what was being proposed. Unlike other provinces, the Island had no crown lands, minerals or industry and was therefore more dependent on the customs revenue that was being transferred to Ottawa than were other provinces. Upper Canada's George Brown said quite incorrectly that under the proposed arrangements PEI would have more money than it knew what to do with, and the Island's request was rejected. The PEI delegation asked for a federal loan of $800,000 to buy out the proprietors. Although some delegates thought this had been accepted in principle at Charlottetown, it was now rejected.

The publication of the 72 Quebec Resolutions on 10 November triggered an extremely bitter debate on the Island. Premier John Hamilton Gray and several members of his Conservative administration tried to defend the agreement. The debate quickly degenerated into an angry and emotional blame-game over who had or had not defended Island interests and over contradictions between what delegates said at the conference and in public. The debate resulted in Gray, Edward Palmer, and J.C. Pope all resigning from the government. The confused and divided Conservatives then convinced J.C. Pope to withdraw his resignation and become Premier, while Palmer stayed on as Attorney General even though he had resigned from the Executive.

Over the next two months the Quebec Resolutions were debated at meetings throughout the province, many of which approved resolutions strongly opposing Confederation. Several ministers argued that Confederation was necessary for defence, an argument that was used effectively to sway opinion in Nova Scotia and New Brunswick. On the Island it had less appeal because there was no immediate or direct threat. Some argued that the Island faced a choice between confederation and annexation to the United States; others rejected that argument as a false choice. Sixteen MLAs including at least one minister made detailed critiques of the elements in the agreement that would harm Island interests. On March 31, 1865, the Quebec Resolutions were rejected in the Assembly by 23-5 and in the Legislative Council by 13-0.

The puzzle of the Quebec Conference, however, was that most of the Island's objections were also valid for Nova Scotia and New Brunswick. While Island delegates fought strenuously for Maritime interests, other Maritime delegates did not. In part that reflected the fact that some of the leading critics of the proposals had not been included in the other two delegations. Confederation proceeded without PEI and Newfoundland, and despite the fact that the people of Nova Scotia and New Brunswick voted against it at the first opportunity. The Nova Scotia government endorsed Confederation in spite of overwhelming public opposition, and was crushed in the next election. In New Brunswick the pro-federation government was overwhelmingly defeated in the 1865 election. Alone amongst the Maritime provinces, Islanders rejected an agreement that did not, in their opinion, adequately protect their interests. PEI would soon have to enter Confederation, after which it would join Nova Scotia and New Brunswick in a century-long struggle to modify the arrangements made at Charlottetown and Quebec City. History would prove that the criticisms Islanders made of the Quebec Resolutions had great validity.

Chapter Four
Yes to Confederation, 1864-1873

The British Government did not accept the Island's rejection of Confederation, and began applying pressure to have the decision reversed. In 1865, London announced that the province would have to pay the lieutenant governor's salary. Other provinces had assumed this burden in return for obtaining control of Crown lands from the British Government. In a bitterly worded statement the Assembly pointed out that London had given away all the crown lands and should therefore continue to pay the salary. Two months later, the Colonial Secretary informed the Assembly that London deeply regretted the Island's rejection of Confederation because it was necessary to ease Britain's defence burden. Later that year, he again informed the Assembly of Britain's strong support for Confederation.

The failure to resolve the land question in 1861 led to the formation of the Tenant League, which may have numbered as many as 10,000. They decided to withhold quit rents until the landowners agreed to sell land at affordable prices. Their campaign was largely peaceful, but some illegal activities and violent incidents prompted the authorities to have troops sent from Halifax in the summer of 1865. London said that the province should pay all the costs. The government replied that the century-old agitation resulted from Britain's mistaken land policies, and it would not pay for maintenance of the troops. On this issue London eventually backed down.

In January 1866, the Assembly debated the Colonial Secretary's dispatch that had emphasized Britain's strong support for Confederation. It decided to contribute to Imperial defence, thus negating London's strongest argument for Confederation. As preparations were underway for the final conference on Confederation to be held in London, the government tabled a strongly-worded resolution saying PEI would not send a delegation. It passed 21 to 7 in the Assembly and unanimously in the Legislative Council. The message was clear—Prince Edward Island would not join Confederation, and no amount of pressure from London would make it change that position.

The offer of an $800,000 federal loan to buy out the proprietors was then renewed. This was interpreted as an outright bribe, and it infuriated many Islanders. It also seriously weakened the pro-Confederation Conservatives. One of them resigned, another joined the anti-Confederates, and another urged the leaders of other colonies to stop making new offers since they only antagonized Islanders. The Liberals won that election with 19 of 30 seats. Another six MLAs were anti-Confederates, and the remaining five signed a pledge saying PEI could not enter Confederation without holding an election on the issue.

Now back in power, George Coles returned to his favourite issue, the land problem. His plan was to borrow £100,000 in London to continue buying out the proprietors. Coles asked the British Government to guarantee the loan and make such sales compulsory. London refused and told him that the solution to the land problem lay within Confederation. London also demanded once more that the province pay the lieutenant governor's salary. That was interpreted as further pressure to join Confederation, so the Assembly agreed to pay, which neutralized another of London's tactics.

Ottawa sent a delegation to Charlottetown in August, 1869 to re-open talks. The new Premier, Robert Haythorne, informed Ottawa that there had to be a complete settlement of the land question by the British Government. In January, 1870, the Canadian Government offered new terms including some small improvements plus an offer to help obtain both the money and the British legislation necessary to resolve the land question. To Ottawa's surprise these "better terms" were immediately rejected. The terms did not provide for the settlement of the land issue, the offer of money looked like a bribe, and none of the province's constitutional concerns had been addressed. Arguing that the province would be giving up £200,000 in customs revenue for £25,000 in subsidies, Edward Palmer asked "if there were three people in the Island who can read and write who are such absolute asses as to make such a sacrifice?"

With Confederation shelved, attention turned to the thorny issue of government support for Catholic schools. The Liberal Government would not provide such support, and Catholic Liberal MLAs voted against it. James C. Pope then formed a coalition unique in Canadian history. It consisted of Catholic Liberals and Conservatives, all of whom pledged to shelve the religious question for four years, to make no new proposals regarding Confederation, and to call an election to debate any new proposals being offered by Ottawa. This unlikely coalition then concentrated on what really interested them - building a railway. It was a fateful decision because the railway led straight to Canada.

The politicians were afflicted by a strange illness that was sweeping the Island, namely railway fever. It seemed that every territory in North America was building a railway. People and politicians caught the fever and decided to build a line. The Island could not, in fact, afford even the interest on money borrowed to build one. It was questionable whether it even needed one, since no farm was far from sea ports. The volume of traffic would be insufficient to cover costs, interest, and payments on debt, so a railway would require large subsidies into the indefinite future. These facts were clearly outlined in the Assembly, where the opposition argued that the railway would bankrupt the province and force it to join Confederation. The government ignored the criticisms, and the railway bill was approved by a vote of 18-10 in the Assembly and 8-4 in the Legislative Council.

The government then compounded that error with a series of major mistakes. The contract contained a clause covering a maximum cost per mile but did not specify the length and the overall amount. That encouraged contractors to minimize the cost per mile by going around obstacles such as hills and rivers, adding to the length of the line and the overall cost of construction. It was decided to use narrow gauge instead of North American standard gauge, the advantage being that the narrow gauge line could make sharper turns. That advantage was not then implemented in the actual construction, leaving the railway no benefit to compensate for the added cost of transferring all cargo between narrow and wide railway cars at the ferry terminals.

Every town and village wanted access to the railway, and bribes were paid to divert the line, each such diversion adding to the length and requiring more stations and loading platforms. The main principles of transportation - short, straight, and economic - were replaced by the political principles of long, curved, and costly. The original plan was for a line running between Georgetown in the east and Alberton in the west. Tignish, however, demanded a branch line from Alberton, and Souris demanded a branch from Mount Stewart. Even before the mainline was completed, the Government decided to build branches that would serve very few people. These decisions added 50% to the length of a line that soon measured some 340 kilometres on an island only 220 kilometres long. Only two-thirds of the line was straight, and 85% was on slopes, with over half that exceeding the maximum desired grade. There was a station every three miles, and provision for people to flag down trains between stations. Engines had to proceed slowly over the torturous, twisting, and hilly route and had trouble stopping or starting at most stations in winter.

Criticisms of the government's handling of the railway soon mounted. When the Assembly met in March, 1872, Pope and his government were attacked by those who thought the line too extravagant and by those whose villages were being bypassed. An election was called for April, and Haythorne's Liberals were re-elected with 19 of 30 seats. They had promised to solve the railway's problems, but instead added to them. They decided that railway construction was too far advanced to be halted. The economy was in recession and the government was facing increasing difficulty borrowing money on the London market where bankers were almost certainly subject to pressure from both Canadian and British governments. Britain refused to help, and Island politicians had no choice but to ask Canada for support. Everyone knew what the price would be.

In December 1872, Haythorne's anti-Confederation Liberal government renewed negotiations with Ottawa. It asked for the "better terms" that the Island had rejected in 1870 plus much more, or "still better terms." It wanted Ottawa to take over the railway and its debts, to increase the subsidies and to make several other concessions. In late February 1873, the delegation arrived in Ottawa to begin 10 days of negotiations. Fortunately, Ottawa was in a generous and forgiving mood.

Ottawa took possession of the railway that threatened to bankrupt the province. PEI received an annual per capita allowance of $45.00. Representation in the House of Commons was raised to six MPs. Ottawa agreed to provide $45,000 annually in lieu of the fact that London had given away all the Island's crown lands. Canada would not force Britain to solve the land question, but it would provide a loan of $800,000 to buy out the proprietors. The federal government also promised to guarantee "efficient steam services" and "continuous communications" with the mainland, promises which would be very costly for the federal government and would become the subjects of bitter dispute for the next century.

Haythorne returned to Charlottetown with the "still better terms" and called an election. The pro-Confederation Conservatives of ex-Premier Pope were miffed that the Liberals had negotiated a more favourable deal, so they campaigned on the promise that they could re-open the talks and get even more than "still better terms." Pope also promised support to Catholic schools, calculating that such a promise would solidify Catholic support for Conservatives while Protestants would split their votes between the two parties. It was an excellent calculation because on April 2, 1873, Pope won 18 of 30 seats, 12 of his MLAs being Catholic. In Ottawa, Pope's fellow Conservatives made some insignificant concessions so he could claim that he had won more than "still better terms."

Having settled for less a few months earlier, the Liberals were in no position to complain. Confederation was approved in May 1873, by an Assembly vote of 27-2 and a unanimous vote of the Legislative Council. Politicians of all stripes congratulated themselves on a nine-year struggle to obtain acceptable terms for submerging the Island in the new, larger British colony of Canada. Lieutenant Governor Sir William Robinson claimed much credit for the achievement even though he may have abused his authority in terms of the small role he had actually played. There were no big celebrations when Prince Edward Island became Canada's seventh province on Dominion

Day, July 1, 1873. For decades people continued to identify themselves first and foremost as Islanders and secondly as citizens of the British Empire. Identification as Canadians came slowly but was certainly evident by the end of the century.

The immediate result of Confederation was that the province avoided bankruptcy. The second was that the railway was completed for the benefit of farmers, villages, and local politicians. A third result was the final solution of the land problem. Backed by the federal loan, the Government passed the Land Purchase Act of 1875 which set a maximum size on estates of 500 acres. That law was upheld by the Canadian Supreme Court and the federal government, and for the first time in history, London did not support the proprietors. A three-man committee determined a fair price for any land above that maximum, and the large estates were expropriated and re-sold. By 1881, 93% of farmers, some 12,736, owned their land. By 1890, the government had used $782,000 of the federal loans, and re-sold the land to the tenants for over $600,000.

Throughout the Confederation debates, many had argued that the federal subsidy in lieu of customs was completely inadequate. It soon became evident that they were right. Even with more than the "still better terms," the province discovered that the subsidy was insufficient for the responsibilities the province had retained. In 1877, the L.H. Davis Government introduced poll and property taxes and was defeated because of it. The incoming Conservative administration of W.W. Sullivan introduced new taxes, re-imposed four days of compulsory work on the roads for able-bodied men, and looked for ways to cut costs, including abolishing the secret ballot because it cost too much to administer. It used money from the land sales for general expenses instead of paying back the federal loan. It tried to reduce the number of MLAs and to abolish the Legislative Council. The voters, however, refused to pay property taxes for the new common education policy which consumed 40% of provincial revenue.

This situation was similar to that of Nova Scotia and New Brunswick. It was a result of the failure of Maritime politicians to negotiate a satisfactory subsidy when they transferred customs revenue to the new federal government. Like the other Maritime provinces, the government of PEI began a century-long campaign to correct those mistakes and obtain larger subsidies from Ottawa. Indeed, Sullivan, the province's first Catholic Premier, discovered that it was good politics to blame Ottawa for financial and other problems. Given the province's refusal to trim the size of government or collect property taxes, these appeals usually fell on deaf ears in central Canada. Maritime governments could not accept Ottawa's rejection of their demands, and continuous pressure led to increases in the subsidies by a series of federal governments.

Chapter Five
Confederation to World War I, 1873-1914

It was very fortunate for Prince Edward Island that Confederation and the land problem had been solved because problems of a similar magnitude were about to descend on Canada's newest province. The great paradox of Island history is that, just as its farmers gained control of the entire island, agriculture went into decline relative to other sectors of the economy. Agricultural production continued to rise, but the number of farms and farmers fell. This happened throughout North America, but its effects were particularly serious for a province where agricultural land was the major resource. There were many causes, some short term and some permanent. Thousands of people migrated elsewhere, and the whole province slid into a relative stagnation which has never fully ended. The political, economic, and social history of the last century centred on the attempts by people, politicians, and businessmen to reverse, slow, or contend with that relative decline.

By the mid-nineteenth century, a great deal of marginal agricultural land had been brought under cultivation. Farmer's costs gradually rose while the value of agricultural products began a long decline relative to other products. Farmers abandoned marginal land and moved to the United States or western Canada. Of the province's 1,400,000 acres, close to 1,200,000 were being farmed in 1880. That number steadily fell until less than 600,000 acres were being farmed in the 1960s. The continuous introduction of more and better machinery meant that farmers grew wealthier but there were fewer and fewer of them. A shrinking rural population reduced the markets that villages served, and the construction industry slowed.

The decline in agriculture was paralleled by problems in two other important sectors of the economy: timber and shipbuilding. Timber production was bound to fall as land was cleared for agriculture. Part of the demand for lumber came from the shipbuilding industry. It flourished until 1880, when demand for wooden sailing ships began a rapid decline. In the 1870s, forestry and shipbuilding may have employed 10% of the work force. By 1900, they were almost insignificant elements in the economy.

Fishing was a minor activity compared to agriculture. PEI was far from the Atlantic fishery, and pack ice made the inshore fishery impractical for half the year. Fishing provided extremely low incomes for full-time workers, and most of it was done part-time by farmers. Mackerel fishing in the Gulf enjoyed a short boom in the 1870s, until over-fishing virtually wiped it out. In the 1880s, the lobster industry boomed along with canning. Then over-production and serious sanitation problems in small and unregulated canneries soon left the lobster fishery as an important but minor segment of the economy. A smaller but more stable industry grew up around the harvest of Malpeque oysters, which became world famous. In short, the fishery supplemented the incomes of many Islanders, but could in no way compensate for the deterioration in other sectors.

In mid-century there was some small-scale manufacturing. It was weakened, however, by the federal National Policy. Though still in its infancy, tourism was beginning to grow, especially as the wealthy came to enjoy a more relaxed way of life. An exciting chapter in economic development opened when Charles Dalton and Robert Oulton discovered how to breed silver foxes whose rare pelts were in great demand in Europe. Some pelts sold for almost $2,000, and a phenomenal boom developed after 1910 with pairs of breeding foxes selling for as much as $25,000. Over 300 ranches were soon selling to a global market, but the outbreak of World War I ended those exports.

The negative trends brought population growth to an end. The number of Islanders increased from 81,000 in 1861, to 94,000 in 1871, and peaked at close to 110,000 in the 1880s. It then dropped slightly to 109,000 in 1891, 103,000 in 1901, and to 94,000 in 1911. Farmers who abandoned their land lost their inheritance and much of their life's savings, though they might have prospered after moving elsewhere. The thousands of men who left were more likely to be the younger sons or people with some savings and a strong determination to succeed. Those who stayed were more likely to be older and perhaps less ambitious and more conservative.

Representation in the federal House of Commons and Cabinet became important symbols of decline. The BNA Act provided for re-adjustments in representation after every census. Accordingly, in 1892, the province's contingent fell to five seats and then to four in 1904. The census of 1911 would have justified only three seats, and in 1903, PEI Island found itself with no cabinet minister for the first time. Many saw federal representation as being linked to other issues in a vicious circle created by Ottawa. Because Ottawa had not provided adequate transportation to the mainland, the economy was deteriorating. That led to out-migration which reduced the number of MPs. Declining influence in Ottawa in turn explained the failure of the federal government to deal with the transportation problem. Islanders believed that having six MPs and a cabinet minister were crucial to the province's future. Initially, these appeals fell on deaf ears as other Canadians saw no reason why citizens in any one province should have greater representation per capita than others. Neither did the courts, which rejected PEI's case. But Nova Scotia and New Brunswick supported PEI's appeal for "fairness" when they too lost seats, and a compromise in 1915 ensured that no province could have fewer MPs than Senators. The Maritimes had forced Canada to modify the principle of representation by population, and Islanders eventually had three times as many MPs per capita as most others.

One problem solved soon after Confederation was the status of religion in the schools. In 1876, Protestant MLAs from both the Conservative and Liberal parties formed a temporary coalition to deal with the issue. They confirmed that there would be a single, non-sectarian school system, and no government support for separate religious schools. In areas with large Catholic populations, however, Catholics administered the province's schools and staffed them with Catholic teachers who in fact taught religion. In Protestant areas, the "non-sectarian" schools were managed and staffed by Protestants who clearly inculcated their values. In effect, the province had separate Catholic schools within a single Protestant dominated non-sectarian system, and one of the bitterest political controversies in Island history came to an end. Language was not an issue, as English was spoken everywhere, while fewer and fewer people spoke Gaelic or French at home. The school compromise paralleled an official segregation in other institutions, with Protestant and Catholic colleges, hospitals, and orphanages. In politics there was an informal quota system whereby both Protestants and Catholics served on school boards and other institutions, and shared proportionately in government appointments, contracts, and jobs.

Having achieved their goal, the Protestant MLAs rejoined their Catholic colleagues in the Liberal and Conservative parties, both of which represented the same economic, social, and religious groups, though not in the same proportions. The great political debates that had divided Islanders over land ownership, responsible government, religion, education, and Confederation had all been resolved. Politics became a battle to control patronage, fought out almost as a form of entertainment at picnics and rallies with music and much drinking. With the great battles over, people became more conservative, slower to react to outside influences. Newspapers informed Islanders of developments elsewhere, but conservatism was reinforced by limited contact with the mainland, almost no immigration after 1850, the absence of industry and hence of unions, strong religious convictions, and the outmigration of the young and restless. Islanders were born Liberal or Conservative, and maintained throughout their lives that there was a world of difference between the two parties whereas in fact the differences were minimal. This high degree of unity also meant that third parties never had much appeal.

The population was almost evenly divided between the two parties, and neither ever received less than 40% of the popular vote. One of the most important political issues was having a provincial government of the same political stripe as the one in Ottawa. Around two-thirds of the province's budget came from federal subsidies, and decisions on important issues such as transportation were made by federal Cabinet Ministers. For over a century, the province elected Liberal governments whenever Liberals commanded the federal heights, and Conservative ones whenever Conservatives controlled the federal purse-strings. Elections were, however, vigorously contested, the outcome depending on each party's ability to persuade its own supporters to vote. The enticements to do so included a bottle of rum, a two-dollar bill, a ride to the polls, gravelling a driveway, and especially jobs on the roads, railroads or local administration. Such patronage did not affect the quality of governance because Liberal and Conservative farmers, businessmen and lawyers were equally qualified to work on the roads or handle government business.

Another constitutional issue managed uniquely was the status of the Legislative Council. Having two branches of the legislature created problems, and pressure mounted to either abolish or reform the upper house. In 1893, the two chambers were amalgamated into one, with each of the fifteen constituencies electing one Assemblyman and one Councillor. Every man could vote for an Assemblyman in his constituency, and for a Councillor in any constituency where he owned property. People went to great lengths to prove they owned property in one or more constituencies, and one of the challenges on election day was to vote for Councillors in as many constituencies as possible.

While somewhat undemocratic, this unique system served Island interests so well that it was not abandoned until 1963. One of its advantages was that it enabled parties to run balanced tickets of Protestant and Catholic candidates for the two seats in religiously-divided constituencies. Parties nominated only Protestant candidates in several constituencies that were overwhelmingly Protestant. But in Catholic areas with substantial Protestant minorities, each party selected a Catholic to run against a Catholic and a Protestant to run against a Protestant. Religion was taken out of politics except that, paradoxically, it was the crucial factor for securing the nomination. The result was that both parties always had Protestant and Catholic MLAs, as did every Cabinet. The system did, however, lead to a small distortion in that the 55% Protestant majority in the general population was reflected in the Assembly by around two-thirds of the MLAs, and the premiers were almost always Protestants.

Other problems were not so easily solved. Ottawa's promise to provide "efficient steam services" and "continuous communications" soon became the subject of bitter dispute. For five months of the year, the Island was cut off from the mainland by drifting pack ice. Communications were maintained by ice boats which sailed through stretches of open water and were hauled over the ice floes. It was a very dangerous and irregular service for passengers and mail and almost useless for freight. In the 1860s, private steamers started a bi-weekly service in summer, but the Confederation agreement enshrined the Island's right to communication in summer and winter. Legally, the commitment covered only mail and passengers, but Islanders assumed that any vessel driven by a steam engine could carry freight, and to them "continuous" meant daily. Ottawa never accepted those interpretations. As the Island economy became more integrated with that of the rest of Canada, and as the era of wooden sailing ships came to an end, a steamship connection to the Intercolonial Railway in New Brunswick became increasingly important for the Island's economy.

In 1875, Ottawa bought an old wooden steamer, the *Northern Light,* but it was not powerful enough to handle the Northumberland ice. In the severe winter of 1881, it was ice-bound for three weeks. Provisions ran short, and some passengers suffered frost bite while walking to shore. The newly-elected Conservative government of W. W. Sullivan made better communications its top priority. He complained that Islanders were contributing to federal public works while Ottawa was neglecting the Island's communications problems. The federal government responded by studying the problem, including the possibility of building a tunnel to New Brunswick. In 1884, Sullivan said that the Confederation deal had not been honoured, that Ottawa owed the province better service and $5,000,000 in compensation, and that he would appeal to London if these concerns were not met. The following January, three ice boats became trapped and the 23 crew and passengers spent a harrowing night camped on the ice in a blinding snowstorm. They burned the mail and one of the boats to keep from freezing. Two men lost limbs, toes, and fingers in the ordeal.

The debate grew increasingly nasty. Provincial politicians pointed out that the federal government was pouring millions into the CPR and ignoring its promises to PEI. Ottawa replied that the two were hardly comparable, prompting the Island government to observe that promises made to PEI were as valid as those made to British Colombia. Ottawa repeatedly asserted that it was doing all it could or was required to do, arguments that it then contradicted whenever it made further improvements or granted increased subsidies as compensation for not fulfilling the promises.

The federal government argued that there was little traffic between island and mainland, which the province immediately blamed on inadequate transportation. Ottawa was forced to increase the province's annual subsidy by

$20,000 as compensation and to build a new steamship, the *Stanley*, which could handle Northumberland ice. In the winter of 1888-89, the *Stanley* made four times as many trips as the old *Northern Light* and the agitation subsided. Then a severe winter in 1890-91 grounded the *Stanley*, forcing the cancellation of over 40 trips. Transportation was now a major issue in both provincial and federal elections. In 1896, the new federal Liberal Government built the much stronger *Minto* and provided further compensation for inadequate services.

In the winter of 1902-03, both the *Stanley* and the *Minto* were caught in heavy ice, and PEI demanded a newer and stronger steamship. Procrastination by Ottawa became intolerable in the extremely severe winter of 1904-05. Crops had been poor, and farmers were dependent on imported hay which was held up for two months. Huge demonstrations erupted, and the Maritime Boards of Trade and even the Canadian Manufacturers Association supported the demands for a tunnel to the mainland as well as new and stronger steamers. Another severe winter plus an election prompted the federal government to build the far more powerful *Earl Grey*. It entered service in1909-10, but the problem of transportation remained a highly emotional issue and was a major factor in the defeat of both Liberal MPs in 1911 and the provincial Liberal Government in 1912. Major improvements were made during World War I when the *SS Prince Edward Island* began operating from the new dock at Borden. Throughout this period, freight rates were also a grievance, because users were charged one rate on the Island railway, a second for the ferry, and a third on the Intercolonial, even though the federal government owned all three systems. It was argued that a single tariff would have been much cheaper.

While Islanders demanded the latest technology for steamships, they were strongly opposed to the introduction of new technology for inland transportation. The arrival of the first automobile was deeply disturbing to a society that used horses for work, travel, and enjoyment. Cars frightened horses and people, moved at terrifying speeds, produced smelly exhaust fumes, and would surely inflict great damage to life, property, and roads. In response to very strong public agitation, the Assembly unanimously passed a law banning cars from all streets and roads. Five years later, Premier J.A. Mathieson introduced a bill allowing cars to travel on roads on Mondays, Wednesdays, and Fridays in those areas where 75% of the voters endorsed the revolutionary change. Five of his own MLAs opposed the bill and one Cabinet Minister resigned. Charlottetown and the tourist area around Cavendish were the only areas that allowed automobile traffic. In 1919, the restrictions were abolished because the feared consequences of cars had not materialized, car ownership was more common, and it was becoming apparent that cars and trucks were economically advantageous for rural as well as urban citizens.

In one area, prohibition, PEI was years ahead of other provinces. The abuse of alcohol was one of the most serious social and economic problems in the nineteenth century, a major cause of accidents, death, loss of jobs, illness, family and social violence, poverty, and family breakdown. Temperance societies urged the public to drink in moderation, and abstinence societies urged people to give up drinking voluntarily. When these movements failed to solve the problems, smaller and increasingly militant groups urged government to prohibit the sale and consumption of alcohol. These groups wanted to improve society in general and promoted better health and education. They also wanted to enforce their religious values on everyone through laws imposed by the police and courts. Many Catholics and Anglicans favoured the general social aspects of the campaign and the moderate attempts to deal with alcohol abuse, but prohibition was in part a crusade by Methodists, Baptists and Presbyterians for moral dominance.

In 1878, the federal government passed the Scott Act permitting counties to ban the sale of alcohol by plebiscite. Gradually, all the rural counties banned alcohol. In 1901, the provincial Prohibition Act banned alcohol in Charlottetown. By 1906, that provincial act had replaced the Scott Act everywhere, and PEI became the first province in Canada to adopt universal prohibition. There were exceptions covering the use of alcohol for medicinal, industrial or religious purposes, loopholes which came to be abused. Bootleggers sold alcohol illegally; moon shiners made and sold it illegally; and smugglers brought it from outside the province. In fact, any Islander could obtain a drink if his desire were sufficiently strong. That prompted a relentless campaign by the prohibitionists to tighten and enforce the rules. The police were given extraordinary powers, such as open-ended 30-day search warrants. Private citizens could charge individuals with violating the law and receive 25% of any fine that resulted. Prohibition reduced the overall consumption of alcohol and the problems it had caused. It also created new problems such as increased drunkenness, because people drank to excess when they were able to obtain the evil liquid. Prohibition also created a serious law-and-order problem, as police and courts attempted to enforce laws that many people regarded as unjust.

The loss of revenue from liquor taxes worsened another serious problem. The Confederation agreement left the province with too little revenue for its responsibilities. In spite of all attempts at restraint, the Government did not have enough money to provide adequate services, especially for education and transportation. This fiscal problem reached crisis proportions in the early 1900s because demand for more and better government services was increasing rapidly while falling population reduced the total amount of the federal per capita subsidies. There was little scope for raising provincial taxes because of the absence of forests, minerals, and industry which were important sources of revenue in other provinces. Obtaining a level of subsidies that would provide a decent minimum of provincial services was the top priority for Arthur Peters who became Premier in 1901. He made numerous trips to Ottawa to argue the case, and brought pressure to bear on his fellow Liberal Prime Minister Sir Wilfrid Laurier and on the Island's MPs. Nova Scotia and New Brunswick faced similar problems and joined in the campaign. The result was an historic federal-provincial meeting in October 1906 in which Ottawa agreed that PEI should receive an additional $100,000 because of its unique circumstances. This agreement raised the annual subsidy by 60%, to $222,000.

Like the "still better terms" of 1873, this was an impressive victory. It was also, however, a compromise between what the province needed and what Ottawa was able or willing to provide. When it became clear that the new level of subsidies was inadequate, the pressure resumed, and was one of the reasons the province switched from Liberal to Conservative MPs in the 1911 federal election. The promise to obtain more money from Ottawa was a major factor in the 1912 victory of the provincial Conservatives under J.A. Mathieson, who won 28 of 30 seats. He sent a long memorandum to Ottawa arguing that the federal government was collecting more in customs than it was spending in the province, and that previous governments had accepted far less than they should have so the province was owed compensation. The arguments were well received by the new federal Conservative Government which increased the subsidy by another $100,000. The provincial government was finally able to balance its budget, and the question of subsidies faded temporarily from the headlines.

Chapter Six
War and Depression, 1914-1945

On August 4, 1914, the outbreak of World War I shattered the tranquility of the Garden Province. Because Canada was still a colony, Great Britain's declaration of war on Germany applied to PEI. On August 5, the first troops left for battle, and thousands of volunteers soon joined up to save King and Empire. They volunteered for a variety of motives; patriotism towards Britain, escape from parents, boring jobs, unemployment, or underemployment, and for money and adventure. Canadian nationalism was a factor, and it would grow with the shared experience of four years of warfare. Women demonstrated an equivalent level of support for the war, but their efforts were restricted mainly to the home front - charity organizations, raising money, and knitting clothing and bandages. They also took over the jobs of many soldiers and proved that they could do them.

The war had little impact on the Island for the first few years. The demand for potatoes rose quickly, while the production of foxes, lobsters, and oysters declined. Fishing suffered from a shortage of boats and equipment. An election in 1915 saw the Conservative administration of J.A. Mathieson lose seats because it had dared to relax the ban on automobile traffic on roads and hinted at softening the prohibition laws. Then in 1916, the war hit home in several ways. The demand for food rose as did prices, and farmers became prosperous. Inflation rose to the detriment of fishermen and workers. A crisis occurred when the federal Conservative Government introduced conscription to maintain the size of the Canadian Army. As in other provinces, farmers were strongly opposed. PEI had the highest proportion of farmers, and it was the only English-speaking province that voted against conscription. The war stimulated some construction, but the main economic effect was an increase in farm income.

Prohibition remained one of the major political, economic, and social issues of the day. In 1919, the Conservative Government tightened the regulations, but with little effect. When the United States introduced prohibition in 1920, PEI became a stopover for liquor smuggled from St. Pierre-Miquelon. Some of that liquor found ready markets on the Island. Poverty-stricken fishermen readily took to the lucrative trade. The tightening of the rules did not save the Conservatives, now under the Island's first Acadian Premier, A.E. Arsenault. In 1919, inflation, the unpopularity of the federal Conservative party, and another attempt to raise taxes to pay for increased services put the Liberals back in power with 24 of 30 seats.

John Bell, the new Premier, faced the same problem as had Arsenault, namely public demand for increased services coupled with reluctance to pay higher taxes. Help was at hand when the federal government promised to pay 40% of the cost of improving and building roads. By borrowing part of the province's share, Bell was able to effect a substantial improvement in local roads at little cost in terms of immediate taxes. The government gambled that investment in roads would soon generate enough gas taxes and licence fees to pay its share of the new roads. It was a good gamble because the number of cars increased from around 500 in 1918 to 2,500 in 1925 and over 5,000 by the end of the decade. Better roads also stimulated tourism, a large portion of which consisted of ex-Islanders coming home for a visit. Efforts to encourage tourism were also paying off with the designation of Anne's beloved Green Gables as an historic site. It anchored a National Park which perpetrated the myth of a bucolic, happy, peaceful, healthy, and contented people enjoying life at a more leisurely pace than that in the madness of industrial North America.

The reality was somewhat different. Islanders were amongst the unhealthiest of Canadians, a fact that emerged with the high rejection rate of volunteers for the Great War. The Government spent very little on health. In the 1920s, it actually closed a sanatorium on the grounds that the public was not willing to pay for its maintenance, even though PEI had the highest mortality rate for tuberculosis in Canada. The situation in education was similar. Premier Bell faced the first major labour movement in the Island's history when teachers formed a union and threatened to go on strike. The province had never invested much in education, and after a few years teachers either changed jobs or moved to other provinces. Even unqualified staff could not fill the vacuum, and 10% of schools had no teachers at all. The strike was avoided by a pay raise of up to 60% which still provided the lowest teachers' salaries in Canada.

Although federal contributions and borrowing had paid for most of the road building, Islanders were upset that Bell had raised taxes slightly and increased the debt. The province had also belatedly caught up with the rest of English-speaking Canada by giving women the vote on May 3, 1922. This made little perceptible change to politics, and Islanders did not elect their first woman MLA until 1970. But no government could deliver more without raising taxes, and Bell went down to defeat to the Conservatives in 1923. His was one of five successive governments that failed to win re-election between 1919 and 1935, a period of instability that temporarily broke the pattern of electing provincial governments of the same party as those in power in Ottawa.

Premier J.D. Stewart's Conservative administration was soon swept up in the Maritime Rights Movement. It reflected primarily developments in Nova

Scotia and New Brunswick, where federal policies were deemed to have destroyed the local economies in spite of the "agreement" of Confederation. PEI was a minor player in this movement, because many of the grievances were not particularly relevant. Nevertheless, it joined its sister provinces in demanding bigger subsidies and better transportation facilities. The federal government's response was to appoint a commission to study the problems and then identify the minimum amount of concessions necessary to defuse the agitation. One of the concessions was a new ferry, the *Charlottetown*, which entered service in 1931. One of Prime Minister Mackenzie King's tactics for dealing with the Maritimes was "divide and conquer." Accordingly, he offered the new Liberal Government of A.C. Saunders a separate deal on subsidies. Saunders accepted it, a reflection of the old insularity and independence of spirit. Unfortunately, that decision broke the Maritime unity that had forced the federal government to take Maritime grievances seriously.

The return of relative prosperity also weakened the protest movement. Potatoes had long been a major export, benefiting from the ideal climate and soil. Isolation protected them from disease, and that made seed potatoes an excellent product. With the help of government inspection services, the PEI Potato Growers Association, and seed potato prices that were twice as high as those for table potatoes, Island exports surged. In the late 1920s, the silver fox industry boomed again, and some genuine optimism appeared for the first time in decades. During the 1920s, a partial solution was applied to the problem of transferring all cargos between narrow and standard gauge railway cars at the ferry terminals. A third rail was added to the existing track so that broad gauge cars could travel on most of the island network. Islanders witnessed the unique sight of trains with both wide and narrow cars wobbling along the twisted railway that had dragged the province into Confederation. This was a temporary expedient, however, as the railway was steadily converted to broad gauge. It was the federal government, of course, that paid for correcting that old mistake.

Stewart's Conservative administration facilitated its own demise by mishandling the main political issue - prohibition. Prohibition was depriving the government of a major source of revenue, and its administration was a disaster. The Conservatives proposed the same solution that was being adopted in other provinces, namely its replacement by government-owned stores where sales would be controlled. That infuriated the minority who still believed that demon rum could be completely eliminated if only the government tried hard enough. The prohibitionists launched a crusade against the Conservatives, and they saw nothing wrong with breaking the law in their righteous cause as they did by bringing supporters from other provinces to campaign against the

Conservatives. The Liberals were fully aware that the laws could not be enforced, but were content to watch the Protestant extremists fight it out with the Conservatives. Under the leadership of A.C. Saunders, the Liberals won 24 out of 30 seats, and many celebrated with excessive drinking in violation of the laws they had just been elected to uphold.

The victory represented a union of genuine social concern, religious extremism and political opportunism. The verdict made it impossible for any government to tackle prohibition for two decades. Continued prohibition meant that laws would be flouted openly and enforced unevenly. It also meant that the government was deprived of liquor taxes to the detriment of every government service. That probably undermined the case for increased federal assistance: - why should Canadians provide funds to a province that would not raise taxes locally as every other jurisdiction in Canada was doing?

The optimism of the late 1920s was short lived as the Great Depression descended on the Island in the early months of 1930. By 1932, the value of agricultural production was less than half that of 1929. Farmers reverted to subsistence living, parked their trucks, and hitched up the horses again, while their wives grew more vegetables and mended worn-out clothes. Visits to doctors and dentists were postponed, and the population grew even more unhealthy. Most wage earners, however, were better off, because prices fell more than incomes. The Island was spared the massive unemployment that afflicted industrial regions, and indeed Islanders shipped free potatoes to the West. Still, the fall in income was devastating to farmers, unemployment rose drastically, and people swallowed their pride and applied for direct relief. This time, out-migration was no help because there were no jobs in the areas where Maritimers traditionally moved. One of the few positive elements in people's lives is that almost everyone now had a radio, and they could listen to superb entertainment such as *Don Messer and his Islanders*, one of the most famous bands ever produced in Canada.

The Liberal Government, now under Premier W.M. Lea, believed quite wrongly that the correct policy to pursue in bad times was restraint. Accordingly, it cut spending and reduced the provincial debt. In 1930, however, the Conservatives returned to power in Ottawa, and Islanders once more followed the tradition of electing governments of the same stripe as those in Ottawa, this time putting J.D. Stewart's Conservatives back in power. Like the Liberals, his cabinet had no idea of how to fight a Depression. The initiative to help the poor and starving came from the federal government. Unfortunately it was in the form of shared cost programs for welfare, with the municipalities to pay the first third, the province the next, and Ottawa the last third. Many municipalities could not afford their share, and the program which appeared fair in theory had the perverse effect of concentrating federal relief spending on the richest areas in Canada at the expense of the poorest, with much of PEI being in the latter category.

The province could not afford to refuse all the federal funds, and it borrowed money to pay its share of new road building and surfacing programs. These projects were made as labour-intensive as possible, and they were welcomed by the public because working on infrastructure projects maintained people's dignity. They were welcomed by the party in power because road construction always provided opportunities for patronage. The old age pension also demonstrated how federal shared-cost policies distorted provincial finances. In the 1920s, Ottawa offered to pay 50% of a new pension scheme, but Maritime provinces could not afford their share. In 1931, Ottawa raised its share to 75%, and the Stewart Government decided it could not afford not to participate. The only way it could do so was by providing pensions at 60% the level of Ontario's and making the qualifications so strict that only 20% of seniors were eligible. A few people were transferred from welfare, where the provinces and municipalities were paying 66% of the cost, to pensions where Ottawa was paying 75%. Figuring out how to manipulate federal programs became a dominant theme in provincial politics and consumed much time and energy.

The Depression was unrelenting, and the Conservatives were doomed to lose the 1935 election, partly because the Liberals were returning to power in Ottawa and PEI was bound to follow suit. Islanders had little reason to believe that a new Liberal government would improve the situation. The Liberals promised restraint and criticized the Conservative regime for borrowing money and spending recklessly on roads. Economically, the Liberals were proposing the worst possible policies, but politically, they seemed attractive. The Liberals won 59% of the vote, and every seat in the Assembly, the first time any government in Canada faced no opposition. The new government, soon to be headed by Premier Thane Campbell, honoured its promises and reduced spending. In 1937, it actually cancelled the relief program on the assumption that the Depression was over. The Depression, in fact, lasted until the autumn of 1939 when the outbreak of World War II saved the economy and probably the Liberal Government.

Canada had become an independent country in 1931, and the Island went to war when Canada itself declared war on Germany on September 10, 1939. Once more, recruitment was strong, escaping unemployment and underemployment being important motives. Canadian nationalism was now more important, British patriotism less so, and the war definitely strengthened bonds with other Canadians. Enlistment was higher than in the Great War and eventually exceeded 6,000. This time, women joined the services as well as entering the workforce to replace men who had volunteered. This time, the progress women made in terms of rights, respect, status, confidence, and financial independence was more difficult to erase.

The war had little direct effect on the Island, though German submarines sank a number of ships in the Gulf of St. Lawrence after 1941. There was some concern with German attacks or sabotage, and facilities such as the ferry terminals were guarded. Military bases were constructed in Charlottetown, Tignish, Mount Pleasant, Wellington, and St. Eleanor's. There was some short-term stimulation to construction, shipbuilding, and repair, but that was not sustained in peacetime. The fishery boomed, and a new cash crop, Irish moss, became an important element in the economy. One great success story was the founding of Maritime Central Airways by Carl Burke. Canadian Airlines suspended its service to Charlottetown, and Burke stepped into the void with a new company that quickly became the largest airline in the Maritimes and eventually the third largest in Canada. Agricultural production doubled, and that put new strains on the ferry services. The *Charlottetown,* which had entered service in 1931, hit a reef and sank in 1941. The nation's shipbuilding capacity was directed to the navy and the merchant marine, so the old *Prince Edward Island* was put to work and a small ferry assigned to a new service between Wood Islands and Pictou, Nova Scotia. These services were completely inadequate, and the war brought long waits for passengers and produce.

Canada's industrial contribution to the war was concentrated in Ontario and Quebec, and thousands of Islanders moved there to work in those war industries. At the same time, many single servicemen were stationed on the Island, and many women found themselves independent for the first time ever. While the morals of the majority were probably little affected, the war did have significant social effects in terms of venereal disease, marriage breakdown, children born outside marriage, and the near-complete breakdown of prohibition. Politically, the most important and curious development was the change of captains in the Liberal party after Thane Campbell retired. None of the experienced ministers had much support, and the backbenchers elected one of themselves as Premier. Walter Jones was a huge man, a successful athlete, a graduate in agriculture, a high school principle, and a highly-successful "scientific" farmer. He was a Liberal outsider who had committed the sin of running for the Progressive Party in the 1920s, and he was tough, independent-minded, and determined. Jones would lead the party and the government for a decade.

Chapter Seven
Boom Times, 1945-1966

World War II resulted in far fewer casualties per capita than the Great War. Problems such as conscription and inflation were handled much better than in World War I, and the war brought five years of prosperity. It was clear by 1943 that the Allies were going to win, and governments began preparing for a seamless transition to a peacetime economy to avoid the depression and labour violence that marked the end of World War I. The war had brought a temporary construction boom but no major change to the fundamentals of the economy. In 1945, people celebrated the victories in Europe and the Pacific, welcomed the soldiers home and faced the future with optimism.

Part of that optimism reflected a sea-change in the federal government's attitude towards economics and its role in the nation's social and economic life. Federal policies had made the Depression worse, and Ottawa had learned some lessons. From 1939 onwards it planned to intervene in the economy by providing stimulus when unemployment edged upwards and reducing its spending if prices rose too quickly, a policy known as Keynesian economics. Its plan for intervention included national policies and standards in a new, federally-dominated welfare state. Programs included the child allowance and a national unemployment scheme. Several provinces objected to these federal invasions of provincial jurisdiction, but PEI was not amongst them as it had long since accepted that it was a dependency of Ottawa.

The influx of federal welfare spending added to a burst of economic activity throughout the Island. Returning veterans had most of their wartime wages to spend. The war had been financed to a large extent by borrowing from individuals. Wartime had produced high incomes, but rationing had sharply reduced the supply of consumer goods. Now people had those savings to spend, wartime industry shifted to the production of consumer goods, and Canadians went on a spending spree to compensate for pent-up demand that dated back to the 1920s. Farmers bought tractors and trucks and people bought cars, radios, clothes washers, refrigerators, new clothes, and better food. There was money left for entertainment and even luxuries, such as a summer vacation. The social change that started with the war carried on as cars freed young adults from close parental supervision, and the prohibition laws became an even more absurd symbol of a bygone age.

High on Premier Jones' list for reform was prohibition. The prohibitionists were still a very powerful lobby, and clever means had to be devised to break their domination. In April 1946, Jones decided to use one of the loopholes in the law to make prohibition pointless. It had always been legal for doctors to prescribe liquor as a form of medicine, and tens of thousands of prescriptions were written for Islanders who had no obvious illness. Jones amended the rules so that doctors could write prescriptions covering multiple re-fillings over a six month period. Two Ministers voted against it, but most of the Conservative MLAs supported him. Then, Lieutenant Governor Bradford LePage, a prohibitionist, refused to sign the bill. That abuse of authority might have provoked a constitutional crisis, but he was near the end of his term, and the new Lieutenant Governor signed it. Chief Justice Thane Campbell then insisted that the legislation be passed again, which further delayed the end of prohibition. In 1948, Jones introduced a law providing for government-owned liquor stores in which people could buy a limited amount under permit. A plebiscite confirmed that PEI was catching up to other provinces, though it was still illegal to drink in public. From 1945 to 1960, revenue from liquor sales increased tenfold, money desperately needed for health and education. The requirement for a permit was abolished only in 1975. Paradoxically, the province that first introduced prohibition and was the last to abolish it had the highest incidence of alcoholism in Canada.

On another issue, labour relations, Jones was anything but progressive. In 1947, workers at Canada Packers went on strike for a wage increase of 32 cents per hour. Jones believed that in a province overwhelmingly dependent on farming, it was unacceptable for less than 100 workers to use the power of a strike to squeeze a pay raise out of producers and consumers. The government declared the strike illegal, seized the plant, and hired non-unionized workers to keep it operating. It passed a tough law banning national or international unions from the Island. When the strike collapsed, the government demanded that the non-unionized workers be retained, which the unionized workers rejected. The government refused to back down, and the strikers finally accepted both the non-unionized workers and a wage settlement of less than one-fifth of what they had originally demanded. Throughout Canada Jones' actions were seen as a violation of civil rights, and PEI soon abandoned the tough anti-union legislation. But in a provincial election, the Liberals increased their majority by four seats, and the pro-union Co-operative Commonwealth Federation or CCF candidates received almost no support.

With the war over, the province could resume one of its most important programs, namely rural electrification. That program had begun in the 1920s but was suspended by the Depression and the war. The plan called for the government to build 500 miles of lines which the farms could then tap. Electricity revolutionized work in the barns and homes, with lights, milking machines, cream separators, water pumps and household appliances. Highway building was also resumed after the wartime delay. Paving was particularly important as there was no gravel, and clay roads turned into impassable mud holes in wet weather. In 1950, PEI joined in the federal Trans-Canada Highway program by which Ottawa paid half the costs of an excellent road from Charlottetown to the two ferry terminals at Borden and Wood Islands. Other federal programs were utilized to pave most of the Island's roads.

These programs barely kept pace with the explosion in car ownership, and gas and vehicle taxes became the most important source of revenue collected by the provincial government. Gas taxes were particularly acceptable because tourists and the rich paid more than their share. The mechanization of the farms, better roads, and rural electrification accelerated a trend that dated back to the 1880s and was deeply worrying to Islanders, namely the declining number of farms. From 1941 to 1961, 5,000 of the 12,000 farms disappeared with a comparable drop in the farm population. Since the Island's population was now increasing, the proportion living on farms was declining even faster. Urban centres such as Charlottetown and Summerside were growing, and these trends were seen by some as a threat to the Island's identity and way of life.

In 1955, the Liberals won their sixth straight election and began their twentieth year in office, comfortable in the knowledge that their Liberal cousins still governed the nation from Ottawa. It was a false sense of security because radio, TV, and increased travel to and from the Island made people increasingly aware of how far the province had slipped behind the rest of the country and how little their Liberal MLAs and MPs were doing about it. In 1957, PEI gave all four of its federal seats to John Diefenbaker's Conservatives. That election marked a revolutionary change in terms of attitudes towards the responsibilities and role of government for economic development. Views that had held sway since Confederation gave way to ones that still prevail. The federal government stopped defending Confederation as a fair, national deal and accepted that federal policies had indeed transferred wealth from East and West to central Canada and that something had to be done to make Confederation fair for all provinces. Co-operation replaced confrontation as the dominant theme of federal-provincial relations.

In Ottawa the change began in the dying days of the federal Liberal regime, but it only became meaningful with the Conservative victory in 1957. One of the new federal government's programs provided unconditional Atlantic Adjustment Grants which allowed PEI to improve the quality of provincially-administered programs. These grants were soon absorbed into the federal equalization grants program to assist "have not" provinces such as PEI in providing basic services comparable to those of the "have" provinces such as Ontario. By 1959, over 55% of provincial revenue was coming from the federal government, but the province still had to borrow money to pay its portion of shared-cost programs.

In the 1958 federal election the Island elected Conservatives once more. Then, in keeping with the tradition of having the same party in power provincially as in Ottawa, the PEI election of September 1, 1959, put the Conservatives in office for the first time since 1935. The new Premier, Walter Shaw, had a folksy rural style that masked a shrewd, educated, and calculating mind. He had spent decades as deputy minister of the most important department, agriculture, and knew government, politics, and the Island inside out. His goal was to close the gap between PEI and the rest of Canada. He knew that the path lay through participating in the many new programs that Ottawa was introducing to deal with poverty in the depressed regions of the country that had not benefitted from previous federal policies. Well aware of the province's inadequacies, Shaw began modernizing and expanding the civil service, reducing patronage, and initiating professional studies of various sectors of the economy. Although it was a necessary reform, the strengthening of the civil service weakened the influence, importance, and prestige of elected MLAs, a process that would continue over the next decades.

PEI willingly participated in federal programs such as Roads to Resources, the Agricultural Rehabilitation and Development Act (ARDA), the Fund for Regional Development (FRED), and the Atlantic Development Board (ADB), many of which were absorbed into the programs of the Department of Regional Expansion or DREE in the 1970s. Like the other Maritime provinces, it sought outside investment to create economic growth, diversification, jobs, and taxes. The strategy was to add value to Island products through investments such as Langley Fruit Packers in Montague and Seabrook Frozen Foods in New Annan. The province, however, lacked the capacity to evaluate the viability of private investments, and a certain degree of desperation led to hasty and poor decisions. Both of these early investments went bankrupt. A bigger disaster awaited Shaw when he started dealing with Jens Moe. Moe Industries planned to establish a fish and vegetable processing plant in Georgetown called Garden Gulf Foods, along with a shipbuilding plant, Bathurst Marine, to produce fishing boats to supply the food processor. Moe, in fact, had little management experience, and Georgetown was not a good site for a fish plant since the harbour froze over for part of the winter. There were design problems, dubious accounting, cost overruns, a huge loss of investment and credibility, and great political embarrassment.

The government was far more successful exploiting the Island's natural beauty and way of life for the tourist industry. This was a virtuous circle: as more North Americans visited, the province invested in more and better motels, restaurants, resorts, facilities, activities, and roads which in turn attracted more tourists. Fiddle music and lobster suppers, Green Gables, sandy beaches, fishing, and golfing were enjoyed by Islanders and tourists alike. Charlottetown got a face-lift for the centenary of the 1864 Confederation conference with a new culture centre and art gallery and a visit by Queen Elizabeth II. So as not to appear too old-fashioned, the province finally allowed restaurants and lounges to serve wine and spirits.

The Shaw government also began dragging the education system into the modern era. Less than one-third of high school students were graduating so the government built 15 regional high schools bringing the total to 24 by 1969. Technical and vocational education received a boost when schools were opened in Charlottetown and Summerside. The province still maintained almost 250 small elementary schools with inadequate facilities and poorly paid teachers. The government began increasing its share of their costs to improve facilities and teaching standards.

Higher education became a problem when the Liberal government tinkered with the delicate compromises that had kept religion out of politics for a century. Under those compromises, St. Dunstan's was a degree-granting university while Prince of Wales College provided teacher training. In 1957, the Liberal government decided to allow St. Dunstan's to offer teacher training, which upset the Protestants. In 1964, the Conservative government began moving towards making Prince of Wales a degree-granting university, which upset the Catholics. The Cabinet and both parties split on religious lines, and those divisions became public. In 1965, Prince of Wales College was granted university status as a temporary measure. That gave it equal status with St. Dunstan's, which was facing increasing financial problems.

The question then was whether the two institutions would be federated into a single university which maintained their two separate identities, or amalgamated in a single new secular university. After three more years of debate, Premier Alex Campbell took the politically courageous but controversial decision to create a single, public, non-denominational University of Prince Edward Island (UPEI). Campbell made a strong speech in the Assembly, and the bill passed unanimously. Religious extremists and both universities were shocked, and some members of the faculty and staff resigned in protest. The Government then implemented the change slowly, and integration went quite smoothly once the finality of the decision was accepted.

In December 1962, Premier Shaw called an election and won 19 of 30 seats. His policies were effective and the province was growing when he called another one in 1966. He faced the disadvantage that the Liberals now ruled in Ottawa, and tradition suggested that more favours would flow if their political cousins took office in Charlottetown. Shaw was 78 years old and everyone was quite familiar with his assets and liabilities. The Liberals had a new, dynamic, thirty-two year old leader in Alex Campbell, son of Thane Campbell who had been a popular premier a generation earlier. Campbell was a handsome lawyer, outgoing, at ease with everyone and, like Shaw, a believer in change. One of Shaw's many reforms was to eliminate the property qualification for voting for Councillors. The 1966 election was therefore the Island's first fully democratic election, apart from the fact that rural ridings were vastly over-represented at the expense of Charlottetown, though that problem had been eased by giving the city two more seats.

In the election, the Liberals gained only 1% in popular vote, but that left the two parties tied with 15 seats each. Voting in one of the Kings constituencies had been postponed due to the death of a candidate. The survival of the government now hinged entirely on the outcome of the postponed vote in Kings, and both parties made all-out efforts to win, producing one of the more spectacular by-election campaigns in Canadian history. The Conservatives appointed one of their two candidates as Minister of Highways, the portfolio with the most patronage to discharge. That he did, lavishing jobs, contracts, and favours on the tiny group of voters. So many driveways were paved that a slogan was circulated: "If it moves, give it a pension; if not, pave it." One voter, presumably a Liberal, put a sign on his front lawn asking that it not be paved. But sentiment had already shifted to the Liberals, and Campbell won both seats. The sixties would end with a Liberal administration dedicated to pursuing even more energetically the reforms that had begun under the Conservatives. It was very premature, however, to assume that Islanders were turning their backs on tradition and embracing an uncharted future.

Chapter Eight

Alex Campbell and The Plan, 1966-1980

Alex Campbell took over a province with fundamental problems that had been developing for decades. The provincial and federal governments had concluded that major change was necessary. Many Islanders knew or sensed that "things had to change." A number of major problems that had retarded growth had been solved. The most important of these was probably the change in federal policy in the mid-1950s when Ottawa accepted that "have not" provinces such as PEI must be given special federal funding to close the gap between their income and level of government services and the national averages. The federal government had spent hundreds of millions of dollars and incorporated much of this spending into permanent programs for the province. Secondly, Shaw's provincial government had accepted that government must take the initiative in economic development. It had modernized the civil service, created new departments, provided loans and subsidies to attract industry, and run huge deficits to pay for modernization and economic development.

All these developments moved the province in the right direction, but the results were extremely disappointing. The Island's social indicators remained amongst the worst in the country, in health, mortality rates, levels of education, unemployment and underemployment, and the provision of all government services. Per capita income was the second lowest at a dismal 62% the national average. The federal and provincial governments had been doing many of the right things for a decade. The governments in Charlottetown and Ottawa decided to do more of the right things plus some different things, and to knit all of them into a single whole. It was known as the Comprehensive Development Plan, the CDP, or simply the Plan. In time it would join absentee land ownership, immigration, agriculture, Confederation, and communications with the mainland as the defining themes of provincial history.

The federal government demanded the dominant voice in the preparations and implementation. That brought a wealth of experience because the federal government had been experimenting since 1957 with programs to solve the problems of depressed regions. In particular New Brunswick had undergone a virtual revolution under Louis Robichaud which involved massive federal support. One lesson the planners believed they had learned was that no initiative would work in isolation from the overall situation. The Plan was truly comprehensive, with every element linked to all the others, sometimes generally as in the positive effects of "better health," sometimes specifically as in retraining farmers for better paying jobs. Secondly, nothing quite like it had been attempted before, so additional effort, prestige, political capital, and money were invested to make it succeed.

The Plan was ready to be signed on March 7, 1969, but the auspicious occasion was marred by the first of many federal-provincial disputes over it. In the 1960s, the idea of a causeway to the mainland had been revived, and construction had actually begun. Costs then escalated far above estimates, and the federal government decided to cancel it. It saw the Plan as a substitute for the causeway, but that had not been specifically agreed. Premier Campbell saw the Plan as separate, and at the ceremony he refused to say that PEI had chosen the Plan over the causeway. The causeway was indeed abandoned, but in 1997 the Confederation Bridge was opened, and PEI finally had "continuous communications" with the mainland, as promised in 1873!

The Plan was designed to create the conditions in which people could prosper on their own initiative and effort. Unlike previous programs, however, it affected every aspect of Island life. It called for the reform of agriculture, fisheries, education, and government, for investment in infrastructure, resources, tourism, and economic development, and for a huge expansion of government services in health, welfare, housing, and education. There were three successive Five Year Plans involving the huge investment of $725 million, $470 million from the province and $255 million from Ottawa. Much of Ottawa's share - $125 million - would be spent in the first five years, matched by $118 million from the province. Ambitious goals were set, especially 7% annual economic growth over the 15-year period.

The Plan was instantly criticized on the grounds that the province was losing its independence to Ottawa. That was the view of the Minister of Health, Keir Clark, and his resignation cost the government its majority in the Assembly. In the election of May 1, 1970, 58% of the voters gave Campbell an overwhelming majority of 27 out of 32 seats. The Plan was the main issue, but the election completed a trend away from the Conservatives, and confirmed the pattern in which Islanders voted for the same party as ruled in Ottawa.

All elements of the Plan were essential, but none was probably more critical than education. All branches of the economy, including agriculture, required an educated work force, but half the population had spent less than nine years in school, often with inadequate facilities and poorly-qualified teachers. It was assumed that large schools could provide the necessary facilities. Within six years, 70 consolidated schools replaced the 380 small ones. They were grouped in five units, one of which was for Acadians although a majority of the 15,000 Acadians were Anglophones and that proportion was increasing.

Education was probably the most successfully implemented part of the Plan. The small schools were eliminated, and enrolment increased dramatically. The larger schools produced more, better-educated graduates. Some Islanders, however, were not happy and a few were furious. The one or two-room schools had been pillars of local communities for a century, proudly managed and maintained by the neighbours, centres of social activity. People went to the same schools as their parents, and watched their children follow in their footsteps. Now, children were bussed to schools where they sat in large rooms with students and teachers they did not know, learning skills more useful in large urban centres. Seven hundred Islanders had served as school trustees but now there were only 75, and parents lost contact with their children's schools. Some of the planners saw education as a means to change the mind-set and culture of Islanders, but many Islanders resisted the idea of being "developed."

Agriculture, the most important sector of the economy, had been in decline for a century. The symptoms included a steady reduction in the number of farms and farmers, an increase in the size of farms, a slow reduction in the overall amount of land being farmed, and a steady decline in farm income relative to average Canadian income. The planners believed there were still too many farmers, working too little land. The solution was to train farmers for other jobs and subsidize early retirement. It was assumed that farmer's income could be doubled in five years and tripled in fifteen if the number of farms was reduced to 2,500 and the amount of farmland increased from 550,000 acres to 820,000 acres. Those figures were interesting commentaries on the Island's history because 1,200,000 acres had been under cultivation in 1880.

The Land Development Corporation or LDC was established to implement the program. It bought almost one-quarter of the acreage being farmed, close to 10% of the entire island. It sold or leased 56,000 acres back to farmers and turned about 70,000 acres over to other branches of the government such as the forests department. The acceleration in a process that had gone on for a century produced a crisis of conscience, the idea that the "family farm" was disappearing, and with it a way of life and indeed the Island's unique culture. Campbell's government had to respond, a complete contradiction of the Plan's goal. Incentives were provided to keep people on the farm, and by 1986 there were 2,800 farms instead of the target of 2,500. Farmers had always supplemented their incomes by fishing, working in the forests, or taking part-time jobs, but by the late 1970s, agriculture was the main source of income for only two-thirds of the farmers: for the others, farming was an evening and weekend occupation. And the income of farmers was still a fraction of the national average.

One emotional aspect of the reduction in the number of farms was that many Islanders thought that too much land was being bought by "outsiders." People were distressed to find that by 1970, almost 100,000 acres were owned by non-residents, including almost 80 miles of the shoreline. In 1972, the Government passed the Real Property Act which required Cabinet approval for any non-resident to purchase over 10 acres or 330 feet of shoreline. Most applications were approved, and within four years another 50,000 acres had been bought by non-residents. By that time, 10,000 non-residents owned over one-tenth of the island. These sales were, however, controlled and the process itself probably dissuaded many non-residents from attempting to buy land.

Fishing was also high on the list of economic sectors that the planners wanted to change. The problem was the same, with too many fishermen chasing too few fish. The planners' solution was to reduce their numbers from 4,000 to perhaps 1,000, concentrate on a few ports, and improve the equipment. Resistance to this program was so strong that the goals were soon abandoned. Progress was made when the government bought back around 180 licences to catch lobster, but that was less than half the target. More progress was made in diversifying the fishery with emphasis on oysters and tuna and especially with the enormous success of cultured mussels. In fact, better equipment and marketing and an improvement in prices made fishing a viable sector of the economy, and it became unnecessary to reduce further the number of fishermen.

The most successful job creation program and one of the most important reforms was in government itself. It was widely accepted that is spite of the improvements made by Premier Shaw, the provincial civil service was woefully inadequate to meet the demands of the 1970s. The Plan itself was drafted largely by federal civil servants who expected to implement it through the Economic Improvement Corps or EIC. They soon argued with their provincial colleagues over the direction and details of the plan. The planners had better technical education and the local bureaucrats knew the culture, but instead of complementing each other, they clashed. The planners' conviction that they knew best cost them the cooperation of Island bureaucrats and politicians and roused opposition, particularly when these "experts" were often proved wrong. In 1970, Premier Campbell had to turn the semi-independent Corps into the Department of Development with himself as minister. Gradually the planners drifted back to Ottawa, and Islanders took their places. In the decade the size of the civil service expanded by over 300% until civil servants numbered over 7,000, making government the largest employer in the Island.

This larger, better-educated, and more sophisticated civil service spent large sums on education, roads, housing, health, and welfare. Social services were passing from the status of charities administered by churches to that of rights administered by the province. As such they received substantial increases in funding, making Islanders healthier and better off. Replacing ageing and inferior Protestant and Catholic hospitals with a secular government-administered one provoked similar debates to those surrounding the creation of UPEI but with the same eventual outcome - non-sectarian government health services replaced religious ones, and another link with the past was broken.

Tourism had become an important and rapidly growing part of the economy, and the planners decided they could accelerate the growth, attract wealthier tourists, encourage people to stay longer, and entice them to go beyond the Charlottetown-Cavendish Beach region. Expensive resorts were built in the eastern and western extremities of the Island. Plans were developed to establish a second National Park in eastern Kings County on some beautiful land that had been largely abandoned. The local population objected so strongly that Campbell had to cancel the project. That local revolt was part of a growing chorus of discontent over the whole thrust of the tourist policy, the emphasis on wealthy tourists, the building of some facilities that some saw as tasteless, the idea that governments could ride roughshod over the interests and views of inhabitants in the name of attracting outsiders who clogged up the ferries, roads and beaches. The number of tourists actually declined, and that aspect of the Plan was a failure.

By the mid 1970s, so many aspects of the Plan had been abandoned that it was no longer "comprehensive." More and more it amounted to the continuation of a number of programs that preceded it plus those elements of the new Plan that were still being pursued. The number of farmers and fishermen had fallen, but Islanders had not been turned mentally and culturally into urban central Canadians. In the mid 1970s, Islanders earned on average 71% the national income while a decade earlier that gap had been 62%. The expectation that economic growth would reduce PEI's dependence on Ottawa, however, had not materialized. Instead, the province had fallen much further into debt in spite of raising taxes, and Ottawa had to provide 90% of the costs of the rest of the Plan. By the end of the Third Phase, the province had paid less than 40% of its share. That reinforced the sense of dependency and cynicism, psychological problems the Plan was supposed to solve.

Attitudes towards Unemployment Insurance or UI reflected that loss of confidence as UI came to be seen as the major source of income, some viewing work as a necessary means of qualifying for the payments. In some cases the timing and length of jobs was determined by the rules of eligibility, and some workers mysteriously became unemployed as soon as they were eligible for UI.

The work ethic probably deteriorated, and a work force relying heavily on UI could not possibly close the income gap with a national average based overwhelmingly on full-time work. Paradoxically, the UI payments which reduced poverty also perpetuated it.

Long before the Government faced re-election in 1974, Campbell had begun to trim his sails to the winds of criticism. The election was fought on the Plan. The voters had a choice between a modified Plan administered by a chastened but still popular and trusted Campbell, or the Conservatives who railed against the Plan but had little to offer by way of a constructive alternative. The Liberals were re-elected with 26 seats, a loss of only one, but the Plan was almost as dead as if the Conservatives had won.

The second phase of the Plan placed more emphasis on attracting industry and diversifying the economy. The method was the same package of incentives being used by other provinces - low rents in provincially-constructed industrial parks, subsidies and tax breaks, and an emphasis on small companies. Although over two dozen companies opened plants in the 1970s and the value of manufacturing rose substantially, industry remained a small sector in the overall economy, and its growth prospects were severely limited by high energy bills, transportation costs, and the fact that raw materials had to be imported. It was not, in fact, economic to locate industries on the Island, and they could succeed only if government provided sufficient subsidies to overcome natural disadvantages, an unsustainable strategy to diversify an economy or close the gap between it and the national average.

These changes both reflected and contributed to longer-term changes in the make-up of the population. One of the most important aspects of modernization was a falling birth rate, and the change within a few generations from families of six or more children to families of two or three. That reduced significantly the outmigration that had characterized the Island since the 1880s. The Island's population increased, numbering over 120,000 by 1981 and 130,000 by 1991, indicating that children born in those smaller families were finding employment on the Island. At the same time, "outsiders" began arriving in noticeable numbers for the first time since 1850. They represented new ethnic groups, new attitudes, new initiatives, new entrepreneurs looking for opportunities, and hippies attracted by the myth of the ideal pastoral life that Islanders were assumed to have lived. The latter were also attracted by cheap land, and ironically, helped to save the "family farm" and the idealized life it represented.

By the time of the 1978 election, Alex Campbell was tired of the struggle but had no choice other than to defend the Plan. The Conservatives had a new leader in Angus MacLean. He had been an MP since 1951, knew the Island inside out, and the Plan provided a much bigger target that in the previous election. MacLean sensed Islanders' unease with the thrust and failures of the Plan and promised a vague Rural Renaissance, with made-in-PEI policies that respected and preserved Island values. Campbell barely won the election with only 17 of the 32 seats. He resigned, and the appointment of a Speaker reduced Liberal ranks to 15. His successor, Bennett Campbell, called an election for April 23, 1979. The tide continued to run for the Conservatives who won 21 seats.

The MacLean Government took some symbolic steps to stop the march of imported modernization and assert Islanders' control over their own lives. One was forbidding the construction of more shopping malls, symbols of ugliness and the closing of the village store. Land ownership had again become an issue, and the Land Protection Act of 1982 put a cap on the size of commercial farms. There was little else to the Rural Renaissance or to the Plan. The people were tired of innovation, programming and being "developed." The MacLean Government captured the mood perfectly by doing little.

Over the previous decades the Island had, in fact, been substantially modernized, and in many ways it had narrowed the gap with the rest of Canada. But Islanders had a tradition dating back two centuries of doing things their own way, be it land ownership, Responsible Government, negotiating Confederation, preserving the Legislative Council, prohibiting alcohol, regulating automobiles, or developing education and welfare systems. They had always rejected efforts to force PEI into some national mould designed by people "from away." They accepted what made sense to them in the Canadian model and rejected the rest. PEI was modernized at its own pace and in the areas it chose. A century after joining Confederation, Islanders still preserved their traditions, their way of life, and their independence. Nothing in their history suggests that will change.

Suggestions for Further Reading

The two basic history books on Prince Edward Island are Francis Bolger's *Canada's Smallest Province*, which takes the story to Confederation, and Edward MacDonald's superb and detailed *If You're Stronghearted*, which covers the twentieth century. There is no comprehensive, detailed history of the Island. This short history is based mainly on the books identified in the following list. There is much useful information on the web, including the *Canadian Dictionary of Biography*, *Wikipedia,* and the PEI *Lieutenant Governor's Gallery*. Some of the more important items researched for this project include the following: J.F.W. Desbarres, Edmund Fanning, Sir John Harvey, Sir Henry Vere Huntley, Walter Patterson, Charles Douglass Smith, John Stewart, and Sir Aretas W. Young. Much useful information was also obtained from the detailed comments made on the first draft of the book by Phil Buckner, Ed MacDonald and Leonard Cusack. The main secondary sources are the following:

Bolger, Francis. *Canada's Smallest Province: A History of Prince Edward Island*. Charlottetown, 1973

Clark, Andrew Hill. *Three Centuries and the Island*. Toronto, 1959

Conrad, Margaret, and J. Hiller. *Atlantic Canada – A Region in the Making*. Don Mills, 2001

Dyck, Rand. *Provincial Politics in Canada*. Scarborough, 1996

Forbes, Ernest and D.A, Muise, eds. *The Atlantic Provinces in Confederation*. Toronto, 1993

Forbes, Ernest. *The Maritime Rights Movement*. Montreal, 1979

MacDonald, Edward. *If You're Stronghearted, Prince Edward Island in the Twentieth Century*. Charlottetown, 2000

MacKinnon, Frank. *The Government of Prince Edward Island*. Toronto, 1951

MacKinnon, Wayne. *The Life of the Party, A History of the Liberal Party of Prince Edward Island*. Summerside, 1973

McNutt, W.S. *The Atlantic Provinces*. Toronto, 1965

Smitheram, Verner, Milne, David and Dasgupta, Satadal, eds. *The Garden Transformed*. Charlottetown, 1982

Warkentin, John. *A Regional Geography of Canada*. Scarborough, 2000

Index